THE CAIRNGORMS

THE CAIRNGORMS

RONALD TURNBULL

PEVENSEY GUIDES

The Pevensey Press is an imprint of
David & Charles

Copyright:
Text and Photographs
© Ronald Turnbull 2002

First published 2002

Map on page 8 by Ethan Danielson

A catalogue record for this book is
available from the British Library.

ISBN 1 898630 50 X

Edited by Sue Viccars
Page layout by
Les Dominey Design Company
Printed in China by
CT Printing Ltd.
for David & Charles
Brunel House   Newton Abbot   Devon

*Page 1: Lichen on schist at the
summit of Ord Ban
Pages 2–3: Pine and birch in
Inshriach Forest
Right: In Glen Luibeg*

CONTENTS

Introducing the Cairngorms   7

Map of the area   8

1   Eagles to orchids:

    the year in the Cairngorms   17

2   History of the Cairngorms   27

3   Badenoch   34

4   Glen More   44

5   Strathspey and Abernethy   55

6   Glen Avon and the Whisky Hills   63

7   Down the Don   70

8   Upper Deeside: Braeriach to Braemar   74

9   Lower Deeside: Balmoral and Ballater   85

10   The Mountain Ground   95

11   Walking in the Hills   102

Useful Information and Places to Visit   108

Literary Visiting   109

Index   111

INTRODUCING THE CAIRNGORMS

CAIRNGORMS – FIERCE BUT FRAGILE

THREE SPECIAL sorts of country go to make up the Cairngorms. The great river glens are quite like what you'll find elsewhere in Scotland, only bigger and better. But above the great rivers are the great mountains, and the granite plateau is unique: not just fiercer than anywhere else but also quite different in shape, in layout, and even in its colours of pink and pale grey. Between the rivers and the hills is the forest. Lochans sparkle between the trunks of ancient pines, and hillsides of bright birch run up to black heather, the snowfields and the sky. The original name of the range was the 'Monadh Ruadh' or Red Mount – corresponding with the White Mount, which is the Lochnagar range, and the Monadh Liath (meaning Grey Mount) on the other side of the Spey. The name refers to the feldspar-rich pinkish granite of Cairngorm and Loch Avon. The granite of Lochnagar is lighter; a particularly pale granite was quarried for Balmoral Castle. The Monadh Liath are the grey schist that makes up most of the Central Highlands. The name 'Cairngorm' was extended from the mountain to the entire range by a guidebook writer called Colonel Thornton in 1804.

Much of the land is already in public or semi-public hands: Scottish Natural Heritage, the National Trust for Scotland, the RSPB and the Forestry Commission together own about two-thirds. Invercauld, Balmoral Estate (owned by the Royal Family) and Rothiemurchus Estate (for the last 400 years the Grants') are among Scotland's more enlightened landowners; outside the stalking season (mid-August to late October) they are hospitable to hillwalkers and other visitors.

In 2002 the Cairngorms are to become Britain's thirteenth National Park. But in international terms they aren't the thirteenth but the first and only. A few paths scratch the gravel of the high plateau; deer have stripped away the trees to leave the mountains huge and bare under the Arctic winds. In winter, blizzards tear down out of the northeast, covering the valleys with man-high snow and crowning every crag with a cornice to fall through. Sometimes they do the same thing in summer as well.

National Park status should put a stop to Landrover tracks and other such developments that make the hills effectively smaller – the National Trust for Scotland is facing the expensive task of removing one such track from the very summit of Beinn a' Bhuird. The great pine forests are already being managed back into a semi-natural state, and the National Park will encourage this further.

Left: The Dee above Braemar, with Beinn a' Bhuird under autumn's first snow

Below: The weather station on Cairngorm records the worst weather in all Britain, with freezing temperatures on any day of the year and 100mph (over 150kph) winds

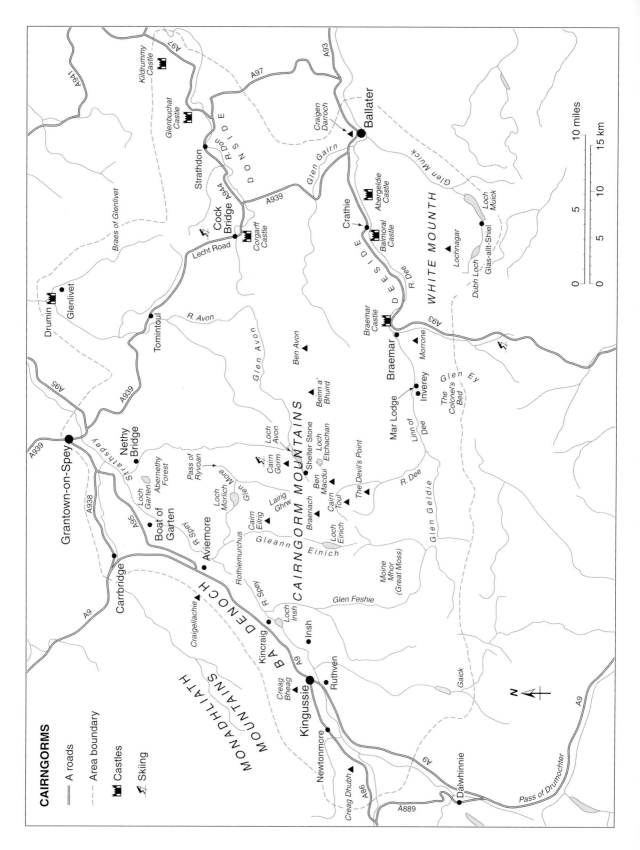

8

GLENS OF THE GREAT RIVERS

'The Tweed, the Forth, the Tay: the Dee, the Don, the Spey' – these are the streams of Scotland, and the last three are fed by the snow of the Cairngorms. Dee, Don and Spey ripple over banks of granite shingle where the salmon spawn. In spring the waters are the soft blue of the chilly Grampian sky, and in autumn the same soft blue is dotted with orange birch leaves. Soft in colour and slow in flow, these are not gentle rivers. In the days before they were tamed with bridges, the fords and ferries of Spey were reckoned to drown a man a year, while the Dee drowned three. During the nineteenth century the Dee carried away its fine stone bridge at Ballater three times.

This is not the sudden landscape of the Western Highlands, but something more subtle. The mountains lie away in shades of brown heather and grey scree. The wide river valleys (strath or srath in the Gaelic) are dotted with small woodlands, middle-sized castles, and world-famous distilleries. Pine trees rise to a small crag, and always somewhere is the glint of the river. It may lack the craggy grandeur of Glencoe or of Torridon, but instead there's a smooth hugeness that creeps up on you. Queen Victoria, who house-hunted the whole of the Highlands, eventually decided on Deeside.

Above: The Spey at Kinrara, just upstream from Aviemore

Below: Strathspey at Newtonmore. The Spey wanders across a wide flood-plain in the style of a river that's almost reached the sea. In fact Spey Bay is still 60 miles (100km) downstream

Granite plateau

*Pages 10–11: Pine forest below
Scotland's finest and most famous
through route, the Lairig Ghru*

Unless fate has placed us in the chilly city of Aberdeen, most of us approach the Cairngorms up the wide valley of the Tay. We leave the Lowlands by the bridges of the Forth, or else past Stirling with its city-centre castle. The A9 was built by General Wade for the pacification of the Highlands; and it's a highway of Scottish history.

Above Dunkeld the Highlands close in: pine trees and lumps of grey schist are overhead, the silvery River Tay below. After Pitlochry's tea-shops and tartan there's a tight squeeze through the Pass of Killiecrankie. You see this well from the railway, but if you're in a car then it's best to pull into the National Trust car park for a wander through the oakwoods.

*Below: Beinn Bhrotain seen from
Monadh Mor. Moss and rock form the
surface of the plateau*

Leaves drip into the river, and match the sad romance of Bonnie Dundee – victorious here on behalf of King James VII (James Two to you English) – but all came to nothing when he died of his wounds after the battle. Robert the Bruce also lost a battle here. At Blair you peer through not-terribly-clean Scotrail windows at the striking white castle, or park the car outside the last-chance tea-room, Civilisation's final second-hand bookshop.

For now it starts to get grim. The road climbs, the trees disappear. On either side are bogs backed by slopes of grey heather, and grey cloud is just above. These are the Grampians, where even the Roman Empire petered out in defeat. When you hit the bleak little village of Dalwhinnie you may start to wonder whether to turn left along the A86 to where mountains are mountainous, crags are black, and places have shape as well as texture.

But Dalwhinnie's better than it looks. There's a warm café, and the pointy towers of the distillery introduce a much-needed note of levity to the scene. And if you stick with your eastern resolve, things do gradually get less harsh and heathery. A new silvery river – the Spey herself – appears out of grey hills on the left, and above the stream is the wooded slope where Cluny Macpherson hid out after Culloden and watched the redcoats burn his castle. Meanwhile new hills are rising on the right.

They don't actually look all that important. Even when you get to Aviemore, all you see is a line of flat tops along the horizon, covered in dirty snow, and with a small notch above the footbridge of the railway. That snow ought to give a clue. Those flat tops are twice as far away as you think, and twice as tall. The small notch is the most famous through-route in Scotland, a wind-filled tunnel of scree and rotten rock, and deeper than most of Scotland is high.

There is craggy grandeur hereabouts: but you're not going to see it from the road or the railway. For this you'll need to penetrate the unique granite landscape of the Cairngorm heartland.

When I wrote my first book of coast-to-coast walks, I needed a special sort of map for the Cairngorms. Everywhere else, mountains were little triangles, and ridges were represented by those black stripes called 'Cathcart Lines'. But the Cairngorms aren't peaks and ridges. They're a wide plateau of boulders and gravel, in all the shades of pink and pale grey, and speckled with lichen. It's a little patch of Arctic transported 800 miles to the south, and the weather on Cairngorm summit reaches an international standard of badness.

Out of this plateau the glaciers have gouged deep high-altitude valleys and corries: the Lairig Ghru is the most famous of these, and the hollow containing Loch Avon the most spectacular. Square-topped granite crags, clean but rather holdless, supply sport to the rock-climber and nesting to the eagle. Green pools hang in the hollows, pools that carry ice from October to May.

No motor road runs through – indeed, there aren't even roads right round the edge, as there's a gap comprising Geldie and Feshie. If you get in here at all, it's going to be on foot – or else, if you're Queen Victoria, on a pony. The price of entry to the Cairngorm heartland is several years' experience on lesser hills, and a degree of physical fitness. It's worth the effort...

In the course of the book I hope to take you into this country as far as words and photos can. And at the end I'll be suggesting one or two excursions whereby the reasonably experienced walker can get a first foot onto the granite. There is also the Cairngorm chairlift – or, from summer 2002

Above: Dalwhinnie Distillery

Below: Frosted heather

Above: Scots pine, bilberry and heather in Rothiemurchus Forest

Right: The beautiful, empty Glen Feshie, where Landseer painted and Queen Victoria rode her pony

Above: The National Trust for Scotland is controlling deer numbers so that pine seedlings, like this one in Glen Lui, can grow in the next couple of centuries into new Caledonian forest

unless it gets delayed, the funicular. The chairlift experience is not altogether satisfactory: it's a bit like being dumped into the concert hall in the middle of the final movement, or having Quark or Netobjects Fusion onscreen when you haven't even been in Windows. The hill-innocent visitor may find it bewildering, and very chilly. The funicular experience, as currently presented, may be even less satisfactory as it'll be a glimpse from the balcony and otherwise entirely virtual and indoors.

PRIMEVAL PINES

On their way to the granite plateau, hardened hillwalkers whiz along Glen More and head up through the ski area – and thus miss out completely on the third sort of special landscape. The Great Wood of Caledon is not as great now as it was when the Romans named our country after it – 'Caledonia' is Latin Gaelic for 'wooded heights'. But the best of what there still is, is here around the Cairngorms. The high pines grow at Mar and Glen Tromie along the Dee; in the beautiful, empty Glen of Feshie; and most of all at Rothiemurchus and Glen More at the Aviemore end of the range.

Most evergreen trees in Britain are commercial plantations. From a distance they're dull blackish green, and close up a twiggy darkness inhabited by two species of bird and various toadstools.

The Scots pinewoods at the base of the Cairngorms couldn't be more different. They support pine martens and badgers, wildcats and squirrels, crossbills, tits, and capercaillie – and they're good for human beings as well. Wide sandy paths wind through undergrowth of juniper and heather. Sunlight gleams through the canopy, brightening a pile of speckled boulders or a warmly red-brown treetrunk. Behind that treetrunk gleams a lochan, and above the branches the hills rise in shapely heather-covered cones.

Among the dark pines the occasional silver birch stands as surprising as a nude in a nunnery. And there is the clearing, floored with bright bilberry, where pines are old and gnarly. The oldest and gnarliest of these pines, that now look down on picnickers, mountain bikers and the little wooden bothy of Scottish Natural Heritage, watched the last of Scotland's wolves go by three centuries ago.

When it rains on Skye or Lochaber, you choose between improving your mind at some ancient monument or addling it with alcohol at the distillery. Speyside too has history and whisky. But bring your waterproofs as well: for a wet day is well-spent in the Rothiemurchus Forest. The wind lashes the treetops, and the clouds above seem intent on breaking every record by running across Scotland coast-to-coast in under three hours. But down on the sandy forest floor the air is scented with resin, and there are dry spots below the branches for a lunch stop. A gap opens, and the lochan is frothy with white waves; the castle on its island drips and is grim.

That's on a bad day. But on autumn mornings mist drifts across the water, and the birches are orange flame against the face of the hill. In crisp winter, spindrift blasts between the boulders under a piercing blue sky, and from the plateau edge you look out across brown lowlands and 40 miles of sea to the snow peaks of Caithness. Two months later, spring scatters golden light across the forest floor. In the treetrunk shadows lurks the memory of the brigand and the bear, and the fairies are washing their green garments in the waters of Lochan Uaine...

Each of these – the great river valleys, the granite plateau, the primeval pinewood – is unlike anywhere else in the UK. The combination is the Cairngorms.

1 EAGLES TO ORCHIDS: THE YEAR IN THE CAIRNGORMS

THE CAIRNGORMS are Britain's largest patch of high ground and Europe's largest Nature Reserve. In the woods the capercaillie cluck and strut: on the mountain the stags are roaring, and all summer long the salmon work their way upstream looking for the perfect patch of gravel. But in the field of animal behaviour, the strangest creature of them all is the one that slides downhill with its feet tied to a plank; that competes in up-ending a twenty-foot pole; and that sits for hours in a tree studying – animal behaviour.

In February, as the gradual lengthening of the days suggests that winter maybe isn't going to go on for ever, the birdwatcher climbs down out of his tree and heads up onto the plateau. The eagle, warmed internally by a feast of deer carrion, is soaring above the corries in spectacular mating display.

March is the best time for winter sports, with deep snow and sub-zero temperatures. Mountain hares crouch in their snowholes, descending to feed at night when the eagles aren't around. A thousand feet (300m) up the hillside, humans on winter skills courses crouch in rather larger snowholes. The human holes lack the two distinctive slots formed by the passage of the ears.

But below them on the moorlands, the whaups, peesies and skirly wheelers – or curlews, lapwings and oystercatchers – are filling the air with the celebration of spring. The haunting cries of these moorland birds are imitated in their Scots names. Towards the end of the month the hares emerge from their snowholes to box, dance and joust in their 'mad hare' mating displays.

GOLDEN EAGLES

These magnificent birds are slowly increasing in Scotland and there are now about 500 pairs. If you're not sure whether the bird you see is an eagle or a buzzard, then it's probably a buzzard: the eagle is much bigger, with a wingspan of 6ft (2m), and this is unmistakably shown by its very slow, powerful wingbeats.

An eagle needs 20sq miles (50sq km) without too much human disturbance. The Cairngorms eagles nest in treetops in quiet corners of the forest, rather than on crags where there are too many hillwalkers and even rockclimbers.

Opposite: Birches in winter
Left: Birches in autumn
Below: Birches in spring (note the yellow catkins)

MOUNTAIN HARES

The mountain hare (or blue hare) arrived along with the birch tree soon after the ice age. As Scotland warmed up it retreated into the mountains; its larger cousin the brown hare dominates on lower ground. In Britain only three creatures turn white in winter: ptarmigan, stoat and mountain hare. Its predators are the eagle, the fox and the man with the gun.

Above: Grouse nest on heather moorland

Even in April the ski-lifts are still running, and mountaineers are kicking and stabbing their way up the iced rocks and gullies of the northern corries. But down below the lakes are ice-free. Beside the River Spey the whooper swans and the geese are heading off for the even more refreshing climate of Iceland, while the goldeneye duck is back and looking for a nest-box. Ospreys return to their tree beside Loch Garten, after their journey of 3,500 miles (5,500km) from the mangrove swamps of the Gambia. Below them in the heather, the male capercaillie has his head and tail pointing into the air, and is making a wooden clicking noise like the indicator light of a rather expensive car. If this isn't enough to intimidate any nearby male, a brief confrontation and flurry of feathers may do the trick. Finally the females gather at the lek – the grouse equivalent of a sports stadium – where the most effectively posturing male gets to mate with all of them. Up on the moorland edge, the smaller blackcock has a similar ritual, so different from the sexual behaviour of our own human species.

In the month of May, spring finally reaches the plateau as the dotterel arrive out of Africa. Unusually, the male dotterel is the one that incubates the eggs: sometimes sitting neck-deep in unexpected late snow on the nest as wind rages across the plateau. The ptarmigan too nests high, safe from most predators apart from the fox and eagle.

Along with the osprey and dotterel, the third week of May sees an annual migration of human beings. The Great Outdoor Challenge has 250 people walking in from Scotland's west coast, passing across the plateau and along the river valleys, and bringing early business to the bunkhouses and hotels. As they pass through Rothiemurchus, the birches overhead are breaking into vibrant green. These bright birches, seen below the shrinking snowfields, give the lie to the idea that the Cairngorms are of drab colours only.

And now the returning salmon are entering the estuaries, tasting the water to identify Spey, Don or Dee and heading up on a spring tide. Shaking off the sea-lice they start a long journey upstream, lying 4ft (1m) deep out of the current until rain raises the water, when they head up to the next pool. During their five-month journey they do not feed at all, consuming their own body-mass to survive. So it's a mystery why they snap at the various flies, spinners, prawns and worms dropped into their path by anglers.

The delicate green-and-white flowers of the forest floor, wintergreen and twinflower, are at their best in June. As the days lengthen, the red deer are heading onto the high ground to escape the midges. For the first few days the new-born calves are left in hidden corners lower down – if you come across one, leave it alone and above all do not touch it. Mother will be back at evening. The calf is dappled in camouflage suited to the forest floor, which was the red deer habitat until recent centuries.

By the end of June the osprey chicks are making their first TV appearances at Loch Garten. July and August are the best months to see hunting birds. Peregrines, hen harriers, buzzards and eagles are working all the daylight hours to feed their growing chicks. The woodland orchids are in

flower, and the bell heather is purpling the odd rocky patch in the moors (the more widespread ling will follow in September). But already the year-end is in sight. The wading birds are departing for the shoreline, and the ospreys are off with their trout-fed young.

With lambing well over and the harvest yet to come, the agricultural year takes a slight break. This was the prime time for raiding into your neighbours' lands: apart from anything else, their cattle would be in good shape for the return journey through the mountains. Today, neighbourly hostilities are channelled into a less destructive form of clan gathering: late summer is the season for the highland games.

Most renowned is the gathering at Braemar, attended by the Royal Family on the first Saturday in each September. Smaller and less formal are the games of Abernethy, on August's second Saturday, and claiming to be Scotland's longest-running of them all. There are also games at Newtonmore, Grantown, Tomintoul, Lonach (Strathdon) and Ballater.

There will be contests in piping and in the stylised and athletic Highland Fling, supposed to represent the movements of the stag. There will be the throwing of the

Above: Loch Muick gleams between pine trunks in early summer

Below: Moss campion flowering at 3,500ft (1,000m) on Ben Macdui

PEREGRINE FALCONS

The peregrine is a greyish-coloured falcon that rather resembles the pigeon in its stubby shape and rapid wingbeats. It is one of the fastest of British birds, flying at 50mph (80kph) and reaching 180mph (almost 300kph) when diving on a meadow pipit or other moorland bird. It nests in craggy ground and hunts across the open moorland.

During the 1970s the Scottish Highlands held the world's only healthy population. Since the 1960s' ban on organochloride insecticides such as DDT, hunting birds have been increasing. Gamekeeper persecution continues, although illegal: in 1983 a gamekeeper died of self-poisoning after mixing banned Phosdrin in a drinking cup.

hammer and the shot. The caber used at Braemar is 19ft 9in and 132lb (6m/60kg). 'Caber' is Gaelic simply for a pole; the name applies particularly to the poles converging around the gable end of a black house. These can be seen in the picture on page 27, and throwing them around was a lunch-break pastime for house-builders. There will usually be a hill race – at Braemar it's Morrone, at Ballater it's Craig Coillich. Unless you've binoculars the hill race is a poor spectator sport and can get forgotten. I once came back from the summit (not quite at the front of the field, it's true) to find myself threading between pushchairs, ice-cream vans and a sheepdog event to get back into the stadium. Most important of all, there's that ever-popular event, the whisky tent.

Meanwhile, in a high cold corrie of Cairn Toul, one patch of last winter's snow still lingers as September sees the first snowfall of the winter to come. Mountain watchers hope that this snowpatch in the Garbh Choire Mor may become perpetual and even a glacier, but global warming makes this unlikely. On still afternoons the sound of gunfire echoes off the hillsides: it is the season for stalking the stag. This used to be a 'no entry' time for hill-walkers and mountaineers, but on land owned by the National Trust the stalkers defer to the walkers. This means that we can hear the autumn roaring of the stags, echoing across the valleys of the Lui and the Dee: the Gaelic poet Duncan Ban MacIntyre preferred this to any amount of traditional harp music. Somewhere half-way between lion and cow, it's a scary and exhilarating sound that once deterred me from venturing out of Corrour bothy to clean my teeth.

The louder roarer is probably the bigger stag, and this can save both sides a fight for mating privileges. Often, though, only a clash of antlers will settle the matter. The successful stag gathers a harem of up to twenty hinds.

The brownish purple of the summer heather blends into the discreet tweedy colours of the Cairngorm country – but October brings a flash of colour. Along Speyside in particular, the birches run like orange flame around the hillsides. Frost is in the air, and the first snows blink across the

Pages 20–1: Am Beanaidh river in Gleann Einich, late summer

Right: Fly agaric at Craigellachie Reserve

tops. Even through rain and mist, the pale leaves glow, with the occasional rowan shading into red. The third week in October is often best for birches.

As the snow cover moves down the hill, the first greylags and whoopers are settling into the fields alongside the Spey. The salmon have finished their long journeys upstream. In the riverbed or in quite small tributary burns they hollow out their 'redds' in the gravel: the hen fish deposits several thousand ova, which are then fertilised by the cock.

The spawn will lie under the gravel through the winter, supplying dinners of caviar for eels and trout. Once hatched they grow into the stage called 'parr', when they resemble brown trout and have a similar lifestyle. After a couple of years they become the silvery 'smolt', about 6in (15cm) long, and head downstream. In March and April they will reach the sea; a week or two into their saltwater journey they pass the adult salmon coming the other way.

The leaves are gone from birch and oak, but pines offer cover and shelter to the squirrel, and food to those specially adapted to eat the needles (capercaillie) or the cone (Scottish crossbill). The spotted red fly agaric pushes up between the dead leaves; squirrels gather fungus and dry it in secret storerooms. Night falls mid-afternoon, and the few remaining tourist attractions close at 4pm. Late-dawning days are convenient for bird-watchers, who can have a lie-in before heading out to Insh Marshes to see the whooper swans and goldeneye.

Up on the January plateau, windspeeds over 100mph (160kph) are common, and on most days the temperature never gets as high as zero (32°F). Blizzards can last for a week. The ptarmigan stays close to the snow-line, and snow buntings fly in small flocks across the frozen ground. And hardy and well-protected mountaineers claim to enjoy the wild weather on the plateau. But as the windspeed reaches 150mph (250kph), small plants are torn up by the roots and even the tough instructors from Glenmore Lodge drop to hands and knees and crawl for lower ground.

The deer too are heading downhill – into the woodlands that are their natural home, unless blocked by a high fence. Humans who follow their example will find the forest strangely sheltered and welcoming. As the gale whips the treetops, and white horses gallop across the lochans, it's almost warm among the pine trunks. The blizzard ends, and for a couple of days the snowploughs labour up the Coire Cas road and the climbers wait for the avalanches to clear out of the gullies. And then there's Scottish winter climbing or Scottish ski – grim sports both, until the day when the wind drops, silvery sunlight sculpts the slabbed drifts, and there's a view right across the Moray Firth to the mountains of Sutherland.

And high above in the clear Arctic air, a speck soars and dives above the corrie. The eagles are out in mating display, to begin the next cycle of eyrie and egg and eaglet.

Above: In the hard days of winter, squirrels come to the bird box at Glenmore Café

SKI CAIRNGORM

Ski-ing is more varied than in the Alps, with such challenging surfaces as deep slush, refrozen snow and bare heather. One-day lift passes cost about £20. There are three downhill resorts. Cairngorm (at Glenmore) has the highest and longest runs: the White Lady is 1,200ft (400m) of well-formed moguls. The easy runs are at the top, in the worst weather, so this isn't the first choice for beginners. There is good cross-country ski-ing in the forest, or on the plateau when conditions permit. The Lecht, south of Tomintoul, has runs which are sheltered, short, and mostly easy. It's awkward to get to unless you live in Aberdeen. Glenshee, south of Braemar, has a nice variety of ski-ing in several valleys. For all resorts an internet or phone report on snow and weather is essential to avoid closed lifts, closed roads, bad snow or no snow at all.

Above: Spindrift flies across A'Choinneach in sub-zero temperatures and 30mph (50kph) wind
Right: Icy Loch Insh

24

2 History of the Cairngorms

Isolation of the Highlands

Robert the Bruce, who won the Battle of Bannockburn and the crown of Scotland in 1314, was a Norman knight. And his time saw the start of the separation of the Lowlands of Scotland, speaking courtly French, learned Latin, and popular Scots, from the Gaelic-speaking country of the North. Around the Cairngorms, Gaelic was still being spoken into the early years of the twentieth century.

From Bruce's time onwards, no Lowlander would willingly enter the Highlands except as part of an army. And the Highlander only entered the Lowlands with claymore in his hand, either in support of a reactionary monarch or else in simple robbery. Seen from Edinburgh or from London, the Highlander was an uncivilised savage, speaking his own language, and barely recognisable as human. An enterprising shipmaster might venture to Inverness to trade beaver and timber out of the forests of Speyside. But for nearly 500 years, the relations across the Highland boundary fault were governed by 'mi-run mor nan Gall' – the great hatred of the Lowlander.

In the early 1800s, the first travel writers from Glasgow and the South entered what was for them a strange and savage land. They ventured into the lost valleys of the Dee and the Spey in just the way their successors of the following generation would be exploring darkest Africa. But by the time they arrived, the great hatred had prevailed and the Highland way of life, if not its culture, had been destroyed in its homeland.

Left: Loch an Eilein Castle
Above: Reconstructed black houses at Baile Gean, Newtonmore

Above: Peat fire at Baile Gean
Below: Both of the main routes around the Cairngorms were military roads built to pacify the Highlands. This inscription at the Well of the Lecht marks the one from Balmoral by the head of the Don to Tomintoul

SUMMERTOWN AND WINTERTOWN

Every Highland family used to have its own holiday cottage in the hills. During the winter, the clansmen lived in the 'township'. The land was farmed collectively, following the runrig system; each family was assigned several strips so that everyone had a fair share of the better ground to plough. Oats, kale and barley were the staple crops. The remains of such a township are being excavated at Riatts near Kingussie; and at the Newtonmore Highland Folk Museum you can see a working reconstruction of a Highland township of the eighteenth century.

On the feast of Beltane (1 May), the township's cattle were driven between the ceremonial Beltane fires; then most of the township's young people would move the black beasts up to the shielings – rough huts of turf or stone in the high valleys of the hills. There, like youngsters going away to college in our own time, they would enjoy themselves away from the eye of their elders while at the same time (we hope) carrying out useful work in the way of cheese-making, spinning and weaving.

Miles from any modern-day road, in the boggy ground at the head of the Feshie river, lie fallen stones in small circles. The abandoned ground is now mere bog, that we would like to hurry through to the tops (but no hurrying is possible in the tussocks, heather and bog myrtle). But 200 years ago, all this ground was good summer feeding for cattle.

Summer was also the time for the principal economic activity of the clans – the stealing of each other's black cattle. The more resourceful would travel right across Scotland to raid the rich coastal country of the Mearns around Aberdeen, and of Morayshire down the Spey.

AFTER CULLODEN

It was the duty of every able-bodied clansman to take up his claymore and bullhide targe (shield) behind his chieftain. Apart from inter-clan feuding that was a natural extension of the cattle-raiding economy, the Highland clans took up arms on behalf of various kings rejected by the English and Edinburgh establishment. They came out on behalf of King Charles against Cromwell in 1648, on behalf of James VII and II against William of Orange in 1689. In 1715, they gathered in support of another James, the Old Pretender.

After that 1715 rebellion, a network of military roads was built through the Highlands by the English General Wade. The present A9 through the Pass of Drumochter to Inverness was originally a Wade road. A chain of garrison forts was built along the Great Glen and the Spey: the best-preserved of these is Ruthven Barracks, that rises floodlit into the night beside the A9 at Kingussie.

The Wade roads, though they certainly improved communications

Above: Ruthven Barracks, fortified after the 1715 Rebellion

between the Highlands and the rest of the world, did not achieve their aim of pacifying the clans. In 1745 they rose again behind James' son, Charles the Young Pretender. 'Pretender' here means simply one who asserts a preceding claim to the throne – the word doesn't imply that the claim is necessarily wrong. And the nickname 'Charlie' comes straight from the Gaelic 'Tearlaich' for Charles.

The story of Jacobite victory at Prestonpans, the march on Derby, the retreat and defeat on the grim field of Culloden Moor and the Prince's escape through the heather is well-known, and not of particular relevance here – a few fugitives from the battle escaped through the high passes of the Cairngorms to the seaports of Fife and thence to France. What is relevant is the battle's aftermath. The Great Hatred of the Lowlander now found its culmination in a deliberate campaign to destroy the culture of the Highlands for ever. Townships were stripped of their cattle and burned, and such menfolk as didn't manage to escape into the hills were massacred. The only thing that separates the 'pacification' from the genocide and ethnic cleansing of our own age is that, in the absence of modern weapons, it was conducted less efficiently.

The clan chieftains went into exile and their lands were forfeit to the English government. The Commissioners who took over the clan lands started a campaign of improvement that coincided with a sudden new demand for Scotland's produce. The industrial revolution was getting under way, and England's (and Lowland Scotland's) growing cities required the Highlands' beef, hides and timber.

MacAllein's raid

It was on a summer's day some time in the seventeenth century that the MacDonalds of Glencoe came raiding into Strathspey. They carried away several of the Laird of Grant's cattle, but sixty swordsmen of Clan Grant caught up with them on the return journey towards Rannoch Moor. When Iain MacAllein of Achtriochtan struck down the Laird's son, many of the Grants fled and the rest were easily defeated.

After a while MacAllein started to worry about young Grant, left wounded in the heather. He went back and carried some water to the boy in his shoe, whereupon Grant shot him in the thigh with his pistol. When Grant found that his enemy could now only stand on one leg, while he himself had two usable ones, he offered friendship instead of further combat. MacAllein was carried back to Strathspey, where he spent a pleasant year recovering.

Above: Queen Victoria's statue at Balmoral

DROVERS AND FLOATERS

And so a money economy came to the North. Rents rose, and were paid by an increase in the small black cattle of the straths. And those whose fathers had driven stolen cattle through the mountains east-to-west were transformed, by a simple change of direction, into those who drove them north-to-south to the markets of Crieff, Falkirk and the South.

Every September, herds of cattle came through the passes of the Cairngorms, driven by small dangerous-looking men. As late as 1859, Queen Victoria on her ascent of Ben Macdui found Glen Derry torn up by the hooves of the drove that had just been through on its way to Falkirk.

Meanwhile, on the autumn floods, great pine trunks were floating down the Dee and the Spey towards the harbours. A special breed of men rode the logs down the great rivers, clearing boulders from the riverbed with gunpowder, passing dangerously under the bridges, leaping with spiked poles across the floating treetrunks to clear a jam. This dangerous trade continued into the early 1900s; remains of the dams and artificial waterways lie under the bilberry in the forests of Glenmore and Deeside.

And as they returned, after a generation of exile in city luxury, the clan chieftains found themselves transformed... into country landowners.

THE YEAR OF THE SHEEP

We often hear criticism of the fact that many of the Highlands' great estates have fallen into the hands of not just the English, but Germans, Dutchmen, and even Arabs. In fact some of these foreigners are among the most enlightened of the Highland landowners – perhaps paying several million for your mountain is an inducement to take proper care of it.

And undoubtedly the greatest betrayers of the Highland lands and people were their own ancestral chieftains in the years after 1780. For the first time, the land, and even the people who 'belonged to' it, became property, to be bought and sold – and sold out. Absentee lairds with city lifestyles made the sensible commercial decision that sheep could earn more than people. The people were accordingly encouraged, and where necessary forced, to remove themselves.

If the drovers of the Lairig Ghru remind us of the cowboys of the American West – if the loggers of the Spey suggest the lumberjacks of Canada – this is no coincidence. For every native Scot living north of the Highland line today, there are twenty Highland descendants on the other side of the Atlantic.

TARTANRY AND TOURISM

Within ten years of Culloden, while the wearing of the kilt in Strathspey or Deeside was still punishable by death, tartan had become the fashionable wear in the ballrooms of Edinburgh. The Highlands, now at last harmless, could be romanticised. Not far behind the first explorers (notably Thomas Pennant) came the first tourists: the Wordsworths, Keats and Doctor Johnson. Sir Walter Scott wrote the place up in novels that were sound enough in their history, while leaving out the brutality and the grinding poverty.

Then came Queen Victoria. She purchased Balmoral in 1848, and rebuilt with pepper-pot turrets in the newly-invented ancient Scottish style. She and Albert found beside the Dee splendid scenery that yet makes no concessions and hides itself behind rainclouds or unseasonable snow at least one day in three – vigorous exercise in the open air – a quota of dubious but romantic historical re-enactment – and a people who took her as she was, with respect but without subservience. In fact, just about what the rest of us have been finding in the Highlands ever since...

Hill names in 'Damh' (deer) or 'Eilde' (hind) indicate the importance of deer to the Highlander. Deer have always been hunted: first with tall rangy deer-hounds and with the bow, later with musket and rifle. The Queen and

Below: Abandoned cottage in Glen Ey, where the people were cleared to make way for deer

Prince Albert made the sport of deer-stalking generally fashionable. Na Caorach Mhor, the Great Sheep that drove away the people, was itself cleared to make way for deer. But almost at once the sport of the estate owners and their guests was being spoilt by the arrival of the first of the hillwalkers and mountaineers.

Walking great distances through or over the mountains was just part of everyday life for the drovers, cattle-thieves and fugitive princes of the previous centuries. It was only when such activity became largely unnecessary, with the coming of stagecoaches and then the railway, that it started to be recognised as a sport. Queen Victoria, on her pony Fyvie, bagged nine Munros (mountains over 3,000ft) including Ben Macdui.

Mountain climbing, as opposed to mountain walking, was invented by the English in the Alps in the 1850s. With the realisation that it was necessary not simply to reach the summit, but to reach it by ever more amusing and perverse routes, the sport of Scottish mountaineering came into being. Close to Aberdeen and the Central Belt, and handy to the Speyside railway, the Cairngorms were from the start an adventure playground for both walkers and climbers. The long walk in, together with the frequently appalling weather, makes the range the most serious there is for walkers; the high crags of smooth, holdless and sometimes rather crumbly granite are cherished by rock-climbers; while winter climbers stab and kick themselves up frozen turf, waterfalls of ice, and vertical hoar-frost.

One day while working on this book I came down off Morrone (just south of Braemar) into the magnificent emptiness of Glen Ey. Snow dusted the surrounding mountains, and autumn sun lay across the brown heather of the valley floor. It was only when I came down into the valley that I realised that the emptiness was only relative and recent. Alongside the ugly scar made by the grouse-shooters' Landrover were the stone rings of the shielings where the young people of the upper Dee lay on long summer evenings watching the herds. They were moved out in the 1840s to make way for deer, and two miles down the valley I passed the shooting lodge, now itself in ruins.

But down along the Dee, Braemar is busy and bustling – even, thanks to the nearby Glenshee ski slopes, in the dead depths of winter. Mar Lodge now belongs to the people, or at least to the National Trust for Scotland. And where once the young people left the glens for the better life of the city, some are now returning for the same reason. The population of Strathspey has increased by 20 per cent since 1970; the new style of workplace-free work can only help here.

The story of the Cairngorms over the last thousand-odd years has held far too much of sadness and damage. At the moment we have to worry as to what global warming may be about to do to this fierce landscape. Still, the inauguration of the Cairngorms National Park in 2002 may mark a turning point for this grand but unhappy land.

This steam-powered sawmill was brand new in 1942. It could move through the forest to where it was needed, and was powered entirely by its own timber offcuts and sawdust. It's now at the Landmark Centre, Carrbridge

3 BADENOCH

Above: White-painted granite houses of Newtonmore

Below: The Fairy Flag that promises the Macphersons victory in all battles. Macpherson is a branch of Clan Chattan, the cat clan, whence the motto 'Touch not the cat bot (without) a glove'. The two clansmen laid aside their kilts at the Battle of the Shirts (1544)

BADENOCH IS THE WIDE upper valley of the Spey, lying between the Grey Mountains (Monadh Liath) on the left, and the Red (Monadh Ruadh, or Cairngorms) on the right. Beyond Aviemore the valley changes its name, if not its nature, and becomes Strathspey. Twenty miles (30km) downstream again, as it emerges from the mountains, it becomes Speyside.

Badenoch is Macpherson country. As the northbound A9 reaches the river, the small but fierce-looking hill opposite is Creag Dhubh (the Black Crag). Its name gave Clan Macpherson its battlecry. Was this slogan chosen by a wily Macpherson to confuse the enemy? There are in Scotland no fewer than seventy-six hills called Creag Dhubh ...

That cry of 'Creag Dhubh' was not heard at Culloden – the Macphersons were out foraging and missed the battle. In its aftermath of defeat, their chief Ewan Macpherson hid in a cave high on Creag Dhubh, at the end of a precipice ledge where one man could hold back an army. From here he could look out to see the smoke of Cluny Castle as the Hanoverian officers put it to the torch. The reconstructed castle can be seen through trees from the roadside, but is not open to the public.

For nine years Cluny hid in Badenoch, while hundreds of Macphersons knew his whereabouts but not one betrayed him to claim the thousand-guinea reward. Once a troop of redcoats under Ensign Munroe suddenly surrounded the house he was in. Macpherson quickly changed clothes with a servant, ran outside and looked after the officer's horse as he searched the house.

On emerging, Munroe asked the servant holding his stirrup where Cluny was. Cluny answered that he didn't know, and wouldn't tell the officer if he did. 'I believe you would not,' said Munroe, 'you are a good fellow' – and tipped him a shilling!

At Newtonmore is the museum of Clan Macpherson. It holds a replica of the green banner that always assured Macphersons victory in battle; and (backup if the banner failed) the Black Chanter that fell from heaven during the battle of North Inch in 1396. Most romantic of its relics, though, is the broken fiddle belonging to the robber James Macpherson.

> There's some come here to see me hanged
> And some to buy my fiddle
> But ere that I do part wi' her
> I'll break her through the middle.
> Sae rantinly, sae wantonly, sae dauntily ga'ed he:
> He played a tune, and daunced it roun'
> Beneath the gallows tree.

A reprieve was on the way but the sheriff put the clock forward to forestall it, and he died on 16 November 1700. The words to 'Macpherson's Rant' were noted down by Robert Burns eighty years later.

It doesn't take much time to tour the three treasures of the Macpherson Museum. But allow at least an afternoon for the Highland Folk Museum. At Newtonmore are two reconstructed farms. There's a 20-acre (8ha) working croft in the style of the 1930s. This pre-war machinery is handsome in itself, ingenious in mechanism, and eliminated hours and months of backbreaking hand labour. The grey 'Fergie' tractor brings a nostalgic tear to the eye of any elderly farmer.

Also at Newtonmore is Baile Gean, a re-created township of the eighteenth century. These 'black houses' have thatched roofs and turf walls. The doorways are low; the floors are beaten earth. Peat smoke drifts through shafts of light from the small glassless windows. Early travellers looked on them with horror, but today's re-inhabitants have found them unexpectedly cosy.

The mid-Badenoch village of Kingussie has the indoor half of the Highland Folk Museum, with farm implements and furniture, and a slightly different sort of black house with stone walls.

Paths lead up from the streets onto Creag Bheag, the 'Small Craggy Hill'. On St Columba's day in the summer of 1838, a party of those about to emigrate made the short but steep ascent, to bid their farewells to their home country. The same day they set off on foot for Fort William to board the *St George*, bound for Sydney. One who remained behind, Domhall Phail (Donald Campbell), remembered them in Gaelic verse.

> Gu'm a slàn do na fearaibh
> Théid thairis a' chuan,
> Gu talamh a' gheallaidh,
> Far nach fairich iad fuachd.
>
> Here's health to the folk will go over the ocean
> To the land of promises: where they will feel no cold...

Above: Weaver's house at the reconstructed township of Baile Gean

Below: Black house at Kingussie Folk Museum

*Above: Fibreglass spinster at Kingussie
Folk Museum*

*Below: Reeking lums as Kingussie lights
its fires on a frosty morning*

*We'll get bread and butter there: we'll get sugar and tea
We shall lack for nothing: in the land of harvests*

*From the hour of our leaving: we pay no more great rents
And there will not be, at St Martin's Day: any blush on our cheek*

CREAG BHEAG WALK
3 miles (4km) on rough paths.

*Start at the Ardvornie car park, near the bridge at the centre of Kingussie.
Cross the small park to its top corner and turn uphill in Middle Terrace.
After 250yd a gate on the left leads into trees. A path leads uphill; beyond a
fallen tree it becomes clearer. Turn left at a tee-junction to contour around
the slope under pine and spruce.*

*The path turns uphill to a trodden-down fence and the open hill. The
small path is clear to the wide knolly summit.*

*A tough continuation is to drop westwards on pathless heather, to gain a
small path along the south side of Loch Gynack. This path goes through a
plantation onto the top corner of Kingussie golf course.*

RUTHVEN

Ruthven Barracks stands proud and floodlit alongside the A9. The small car park is reached from the centre of Kingussie by a lane passing under the main road.

Although the Wolf of Badenoch had a stronghold here, the present ruin is the remains of a castle built in 1722. With other forts at Glenelg, Fort William and Inverness, all linked by General Wade's roads, this was meant to let the Hanoverian army keep control of the Highlands after the rising of 1715.

In February of 1756 twelve men under a sergeant held it against Prince Charlie for three days, and were granted an honourable capitulation. And here, two days after Culloden, there gathered the remnant of the Jacobite army. The passes leading into Badenoch were easy to defend; the army, which had been reinforced with the Grants, Macphersons and others who had missed the battle, was in good heart and ready to fight on.

But the Prince himself was not. 'Let everyone seek his own safety in the best way he can.'

Below: Ruthven Barracks: an after-dark visit by floodlight is particularly eerie and romantic

Pages 38–9: Ruthven Barracks at dawn, with Monadhliath mountains behind

INSH MARSHES WALK

2 miles (3km) on easy paths

*For those who want a pleasant
stroll involving absolutely no
4,000ft peaks, the 2-mile (3km)
trail through the reserve will take
about an hour. The dedicated
birdwatcher, wanting to spot osprey
or red-breasted merganser, aware
that the icterine warbler may just
be attempting to breed, could take
much, much longer.*

*There's a car park at a bend in
the B970 a mile east of Ruthven
Barracks. The trail, which is clearly
marked, runs roughly east to reach
the Tromie opposite Tromie Mills,
then loops back.*

*Unless you lingered after that
icterine warbler, there should be
time for a visit to Ruthven Barracks
as well.*

The Chevalier de Johnstone recorded the scene before himself fleeing through the Cairngorms to the seaports of Fife. 'No one could tell whether the scaffold would not be his fate. The Highlanders gave vent to their grief in wild howlings and lamentations; the tears flowed down their cheeks when they thought that their country was now at the discretion of the Duke of Cumberland, whilst they and their children would be reduced to slavery and plunged without resource in a state of remedyless distress.'

INSH MARSHES

Nature would have the Spey's wide flood plain as a place of tussock grasses and dense willow scrub; man has tamed it with field drains. At Insh, the RSPB have recreated a half-way stage. They've blocked the field drains, but at the same time allowed cattle and sheep to graze in a carefully controlled pattern. The 3sq miles (7sq km) of fertile wetland are home to over a hundred species of birds, 400 flowering plants, squirrels, pine martens, otters and roe deer.

Over the winter, 200 whooper swans drop in from Iceland. In spring it's a showplace for wild geese and the country's largest population of goldeneye duck. In early summer the air is noisy with curlew, lapwing, oystercatcher and plover.

Once a month through the summer there's a guided wildlife walk through the reserve, and other outings concentrate on wildflowers or fungi, or listen to the midnight cry of the spotted crake.

DANGERS OF THE GAICK

Before Wade's road across Drumochter, a higher but more direct route was used from Atholl to Badenoch. The Gaick Pass emerges to the Spey along the pleasantly wooded Glen Tromie, but at the head of the valley the way passes between steep forbidding hills.

Here a dreadful fate befell John Macpherson, known as the 'Black Officer', and notorious for his unscrupulous methods of recruitment into the army of King George. He would make men drunk, then slip the King's shilling into their pocket; or trick them into putting on the fine red coat to impress the ladies at a ball.

In a cabin at the head of Gaick, there came a midnight knocking at the door and a call for Black Macpherson. 'Tonight is the night,' said the strange voice outside. 'It is not,' Macpherson was heard to reply, 'but a year from tonight.'

But a few days later, on Christmas Day of 1800, a great blizzard fell on Gaick. When men came up the pass they found the hut torn to pieces. The bodies of Macpherson and his companions were scattered across the hillside, their clothes torn from them and their guns bent and twisted by whatever sinister force had struck the bothy.

Witchcraft, or the Devil? Today there's a new theory. Though largely unobserved until the recent upsurge in winter climbing, avalanches are not uncommon on Scotland's hills. A huge slide of wet snow off the thousand-foot (300m) slope above the pass could have caused just the damage described, and the Black Officer and his companions are Scotland's first recorded avalanche victims.

Serious evildoers might do well to choose a different route into Badenoch. Another who came to a miserable end here was Black Walter Comyn. He'd given orders that on the day of his return from Atholl, all the young women of Kingussie were to work in the fields stark naked.

But he never arrived. It's been suggested that two of the girls concerned had mothers who were versed in witchcraft. His horse reached Ruthven, with one foot and leg of Black Walter dangling from the stirrup. And up in Gaick they found the rest of him, being torn to bits by eagles...

GLEN FESHIE

The next valley to run in from the south has no sinister legends, and no visitor attractions apart from some short walks laid out by the Forestry Commission. Below the scattered pines of Glen Feshie the deer have grazed away the undergrowth to leave short cropped grass. It could be a genteel country park, apart from the great river that sparkles between the branches and occasionally rushes in flood to leave whole trees scattered across the valley floor.

Above, the first ramparts of the Cairngorms rise in a heather wall 2,500ft (750m) high. At the valley's head the river rises gradually between cliffs splashed with green birch onto bare moor. After another 20 miles (30km) the path drops among trees again at the head of the River Dee: for this is the first of the great through routes. But here below the mountaintops and the moor is this place of gentle beauty. Queen Victoria stopped for a picnic here on her first Great Expedition, and Landseer painted a fresco inside a bothy that only fell down in the last fifty years. The one remaining building is now a shelter for mountain people, and if you step out quietly at dawn the river will be chuckling gently and the deer will be grazing all around.

RETURNING TO THE SPEY

From Feshiebridge a quiet road runs along the south side of the valley, passing Ruthven Barracks and the Insh Marshes. It runs under mixed woodland, with occasional glimpses of the river on the left, the mountains on the right.

Loch Insh is hidden behind the trees, but a turn down

GLEANN FEISIDH NA SIANTAN!

Glen Feshie of the storm-winds
Within your shelter I would wish
*   to be;*
Where I could find the bilberry
The cloudberry and the blackberry –
Round nuts on the hazels,
And red fish in the falls.

Gaelic verse recorded 1906

Below: Feshie bothy

left takes you to the watersports centre and the beautifully situated church that looks out across the water. It was known as the 'Swans' Chapel' because of the whooper swans that gather below during the winter. The church itself is eighteenth century, though its bell is 1,000 years old. Church of Scotland services are held every Sunday.

After Kincraig there's a quiet woodland road on either side of the Spey as well as the ugly A9. The mountains draw closer now, a steep wall of pines topped with heather and bare stones. Aviemore is just ahead, and the entry to the big hills.

HIGHLAND WILDLIFE PARK

On a sunny slope above Loch Insh is the Highland Wildlife Park. Here you can drive your car past the bison that really ought to live in the Rothiemurchus Forest, and look down on wolves from a high walkway. The Park also has lynx, beaver and the extinct wild horse of Scotland.

Many of the creatures that do still live wild in the forest are very hard for the casual visitor to spot – and in some cases, like the capercaillie, are best left undisturbed anyway. The Park is your best chance to see the wildcat, pine marten, otter and eagle. The park is open year-round, though in winter the last entry is at 2pm.

Right: The wolf pack at the Highland Wildlife Park. Wolfpack gossip is on the Kincraig website. The pale wolf to left of the birch trunk is Tor, the current alpha (top) wolf. The fairly pale wolf in front of the birch trunk is Dubh, the alpha female. At the top of the hill is Teine, whose tail was broken by a bite from Tor: Tiene has now moved up to beta wolf and Tor is getting anxious...

4 GLEN MORE

Above: Unless you count the 4,000-year-old ring cairn (in a housing estate at the northern edge of the village) Aviemore has just one attractive building. The railway station was built in 1898 and restored 100 years later in purple and pink. In 1929 William Baxter invented Baxters' famous Royal Game Soup here, when he tripped over some sacks of venison on the darkened platform

Right: Birch pool, Craigellachie Reserve

A T AVIEMORE a short, stubby side-valley leaves the Spey. Glen More is the one place where craggy corries come within seeing distance of fields, roads and restaurants. Add a loch to reflect those corries in, and the biggest real forest in all Scotland, and it's not surprising that this should be the main jumping-off point for walkers and climbers, the sitting-in-cars-and-looking-at-it place for the rest of us.

It's natural to drive in from Aviemore through the forest, decide against the audio-visuals at Glenmore (there's a parking charge) and end up at the car park below the ski slopes. There's a pretty good view, and it's rather charming the way the reindeer come and hassle you for sandwiches. On the other hand, it gets chilly at 2,000ft (600m), and there is only so much fun you can have in a car park. So you wonder whether to go for the chairlift – or, from 2002, for the funicular.

We'll go for the funicular in due course. But first we'll go back to the beginning and start again more slowly. There's more – much more – to Glenmore.

AVIEMORE

Aviemore started life as a timber town. Later it became a staging-post on the long cold road to Inverness. We could compare today's village with a semi-wild forest: the high canopy of concrete hotels and conference centres, with a healthy understorey of small shops and eating-places, and a varied wildlife of birdwatchers and ski-ers, motorists and mountaineers.

After using the useful Safeway store and informative Information Centre, but before heading out to Loch Morlich, pause. The Strathspey Railway is 5 miles (8km) of full-sized steam train; it runs throughout the summer and the return journey takes only fifty minutes. And above Aviemore on the eastern side is the Craigellachie birch wood.

CRAIGELLACHIE

The pre-historic Highlands had a birchwood economy. Even in the eighteenth century, Thomas Pennant on his Tour of Scotland found birch being used for house-building, farm implements and cartwheels. In the townships they sat at birchwood fires, wearing boots whose leather was tanned with birch bark. And on those occasions when the birch trees had failed to conceal the whisky still from the gaugers, they drank a wine made from birch sap.

On the slopes of the mountains the natural forest is the pine; in the valleys of the south and the warmer west, it's oak mixed with hazel. But here alongside the Spey, the wildwood is the birch with her white trunk and dancing leaves.

The smooth granite mountains, and the dark pines at their foot, have a noble austerity. Craigellachie with its birches is made of a different rock – schist – and has a different sort of beauty, small-scale and rugged. Clan Grant in fierce affection took its name for their battle-cry: 'Seas buan, Creag Eileachaidh' (Stand fast, Craigellachie).

The short (but rather steep) trail through the birches is good at any time, but best in the third week in October when the leaves flame in orange-gold. In mid-May again, the leaves are bright golden-green.

Crossing the Spey into Glen More, we come first to Inverdruie, where there is a cluster of shops selling Scottishware and the Information Centre of Rothiemurchus Estate. Two miles to the south is a small loch that some call the most beautiful in all Scotland.

LOCH EN EILEIN

It's the birch-and-pine forest around it, the mountains above and the castle in the middle that make this loch, barely more than a mile (1.5km) in length, so special. Around it runs a path whose every footstep is a delight, even (or especially) in foul weather when wind whips the treetops and the waters of the loch.

The castle was probably built by the Red Comyn, he whose murder at Dumfries by Robert the Bruce set off the Scottish War of Independence. It sheltered Alexander Stewart, bastard son of Robert II and known as the Wolf of Badenoch. There was a concealed causeway leading out to it in zigzags, just below the surface.

The Chiefs of Grant gained possession of Rothiemurchus in the 1570s and rebuilt the castle. The wife of one of them, Grizzel Mhor, held the island against King George's General Buchan in 1690 – and the Grants still hold the whole of Rothiemurchus.

The ruined castle was one of the last nesting sites in Scotland for the osprey. One enthusiastic collector swam out through the freezing water

CRAIGELLACHIE WALK
3½ miles (5km) on waymarked trail (longer route)

The Nature Reserve is signed from Aviemore station and from the Tourist Information Centre. Paths converge onto a tunnel under the main A9. The Nature Reserve sign marks the start of two waymarked trails, with Green Trail 1½ hours, Yellow 45 minutes. The entire route is under trees.

Keep ahead at the first fork (where a path on the right runs down to a lochan). A signed path climbs left past a viewpoint. The path ascends through birches, with views over Aviemore to high Cairngorms. It divides; the shorter Yellow Trail drops to the right, while the Green climbs further to a path junction below a fenced enclosure, where it too turns down right.

The paths return past two attractive reservoirs.

WALK AROUND LOCH AN EILEIN
4 miles (6km) on good paths

The walk around Loch an Eilein starts from the Interpretation Centre and is on clear, wide paths. If the narrower path round Loch Gamhna is included, the walk is of 4 miles (6km) and takes about 2 hours. The Gamhna path is rather boggy at one point.

Opposite: Loch an Eilein in January, with its island castle

47

LOCH AN EILEIN
AND ORD BAN WALK

*Combine walks around both lochs
for a route of 4½ miles (7km)*

*There's a car park near the foot of
Loch an Eilein. From its end, a
stone-built path leads towards a
small interpretation centre. Just
before this, a ladder stile on the
right is the route for Ord Ban. Turn
back right for 50yd, until a small
path on the left zig-zags up through
the trees. This becomes clearer, and
climbs to open heather and the
summit trig point.*

*A path runs down southwest,
keeping to left of a fenced plantation
to a gate with primitive stile at grid
ref 887078. Pathless wood leads
down to the lochside path.*

*Above: Capercaillie at the Highland
Wildlife Park*

wearing nothing but his cap, which he used to carry the eggs on the return journey. Egg-collectors are now, happily, almost extinct; while the osprey has returned to Loch Garten, 7 miles (11km) to the north.

Though only 1,404ft (428m) high, Ord Ban is an interesting ascent through the birches with a truly outstanding view over the loch, the forest, the Cairngorms and (in the other direction) the River Spey.

ROTHIEMURCHUS FOREST

From Loch an Eilein to Glenmore Lodge it's trees all the way: majestic pines and bright birches. The paths below are sandy rather than stony, and well-signposted on the whole. Pine martens run along the branches, though you'd have to be very lucky to spot one. Red squirrels are less rare.

What makes this sort of forest so attractive is its open nature. The pine trunks are wide-spaced, and enough light gets through to support a flourishing understorey of bilberry and juniper, with woodland plants such as creeping lady's-tresses orchid, wintergreen, and twayblade. These woodland flowers are not showy, but have most fascinating shapes. And high among the pine needles lurks one of Britain's strangest birds.

CAPERCAILLIE

What does the large grouse of Rothiemurchus have in common with the whale? The answer is as odd as the question. Like the whale, the male Capercaillie communicates using low frequencies that humans cannot hear – but that are audible to other capercaillie miles away across the forest.

The capercaillie is one of only two birds whose English name is in Gaelic. 'Capull-coille' means 'horse of the woods'. The part of the call that we do hear resembles the hooves of a trotting horse.

This magnificent bird became extinct once in Scotland; and now, sadly, seems set to become extinct again. After its reintroduction from Sweden in 1837 it increased to about 20,000 birds, but has now fallen to less than 1,500. There are several reasons for its decline. Its forest habitat is now very small. Overgrazing by deer has removed much of the bilberry, cowberry and heather needed both for feeding and for concealment from foxes, peregrines and eagles. Young birds die by flying into fences. The adult bird needs to eat about 600g of pine needles (one-seventh of its own weight) during every one of the short days of winter, and constant disturbance by trail bikers or ski-ers can slowly starve it to death.

At this very last moment, the bird may be saved. Control of deer is restoring the understorey, and allowing deer fences to be taken down. The Wildlife Park at Kincraig is breeding captive caper, and successfully releasing them back into the wild. While in April and May the Loch Garten Osprey Centre opens at dawn for a rare chance actually to see the caper's mating display called the 'lek', half cockfight and half Highland dance.

CORRIE FORMATION

The road passes Loch Morlich, where two car parks offer views across the water to the entire northern scarp of the Cairngorms, 5 miles away and 3,000ft above (8km/900m).

The hill edge above is scalloped into a series of the hollows called corries – Gaelic 'coire', meaning a cauldron. From the left, Coire na Ciste (Corrie of the Chest or Coffin) and Coire Cas (Steep Corrie) have the ski-tows; then Coire an t-Sneachda (Corrie of the Snows) and Coire an Lochain (lochan is a small loch) before the sloping valley of Lurcher's Gully and the pointed Lurcher's Crag.

Corries are a feature of all glaciated mountain country. With prevailing winds from the southwest, snow drifts onto north and east slopes; here, on the shady side of the hill, it builds up to form small but vigorous corrie glaciers.

The melting of the corrie glacier typically leaves a steep head wall, and a flat floor which often has a lochan. Coire an Lochain and Coire an t-Sneachda have summer and winter climbing on their back crags. Between them, ice grinding from both sides has left a narrow rock ridge, the Fiacaill, which is an easy but exciting scramble.

At the head of the loch is the settlement of Glenmore, which has a youth hostel, small shop and the Forestry Commission information centre. This is the start-point for colour-coded trails through the forest.

THE RED HAND

Bodach Lamh-dhearg, the red-handed spectre, haunts the Rothiemurchus forest in the shape of an old man in grey plaid with one bloodstained hand. In 1669 he challenged three brothers in the forest, killing them all.

If you do meet this sinister figure, it may pay to be polite. He stole two knives from Stewart of Kincardine, but returned them when Stewart apologised for killing the deer of Glen More.

Below: Sunset light on the Lairig Ghru

49

SCOTTISH REINDEER

As the ice retreated, reindeer came up into Scotland along with the birch trees. They became extinct during a warm spell around 6500BC.

Then on a crisp April day in 1947, Mikel Utsi stood on the footbridge at Aviemore station and noticed how similar was the scenery to Swedish Lapland. Exploring further, he found a vacant ecological niche. The abundant lichen of ground, rock and tree wasn't being eaten by anything; there was room here for reindeer.

His herd now numbers around 150, ranging freely to the summit of Cairngorm. It's a commercial herd, yielding meat and hides, hair for fine fabrics and horn for carving. But the half-tame animals are attractive in their own right. Visits to the herd run from the Reindeer Centre (weather permitting) on every day of the year – except one.

After their heavy workload the night before, the animals need a rest from visitors on Christmas Day.

THE PASS OF RYVOAN

One of Glenmore's paths leads out northeast through a narrow gap – the Pass of Ryvoan. This is a meltwater channel, carved by a river when the obvious way out of Glen More was blocked by ice. It now harbours the Lochan Uaine, which is, as its name implies, a Green Lochan. This is a love-

Above: Crossing of the River Nethy on the Lairig an Laoigh cattle-drovers' route behind Ryvoan

Left: 'Cairn Gorm' means blue or blue-green hill. Corrie Cas (for skiers) and Coire an Lochan (for climbers) rise above Loch Morlich

RATHAD NAM MEIRLEACH: THE THIEVES' ROAD

Ryvoan is the endpoint of the caterans' (cattle-thieves') road. This path came out of Lochaber by Dalwhinnie and Glen Feshie, and avoided the populous Spey Valley by creeping through Rothiemurchus Forest. At Ryvoan the raiders paused to choose which of the rich lands of Aberdeen or Moray to rob.

A letter of 1645 from road-user Allan Cameron of Locheil to Grant of Rothiemurchus apologises for injuring one of his people, but mistook him for a Morayman. The raid was intended to be to 'Morayland, quhair all men taks their prey'.

The old path can still be followed along the south shore of Loch an Eilein; it continued by the Cairngorm Club Footbridge and the south side of Loch Morlich.

ly spot, and the trail leading to it (from the bridge over the Allt Mor at the head of Loch Morlich) has interesting information about the plantlife. So the only reason for not going there is that one might meet the fairies, who wash their green clothes in this small lake. Scottish fairies – the sith, pronounced shee – are bloodthirsty and dangerous. Robin Oig, a Glenmore hunter, came across a green-clad fairy playing the pipes. So sweet was the music that Oig grabbed the pipes, throwing down his bonnet in exchange – only to find in his hand a puffball with four blades of grass. It's best not to wear green yourself when visiting the pass, as this is known to annoy them. If walking with friends, do not speak their names aloud until safely out from under the trees.

Beyond the pass is the stalkers' bothy of Ryvoan, which has been an informal shelter for walkers for over a century. This is maintained by the Mountain Bothies Association in clean but spartan state – wooden furniture tends to end up in flames in the fireplace.

> *And again in the dusk of evening*
> *I shall find once more alone*
> *The waters of the Green Loch*
> *And the bothy of Ryvoan.*

You can read the rest of the anonymous verse at the bothy itself, where it was first found during World War II.

CCC CONTROVERSY

Back in 1931, Sterling was to be strengthened by persuading ski-ers to take their Alpine holiday in Scotland. Hotels installed central heating, Swiss instructors came to Braemar, fields were flooded for skating.

Alas, when Christmas came the skating ponds had melted and there was no snow. And since 1961 it's been much the same story for the ski enterprise in the corries of Cairngorm.

In the 1970s, the Chairlift Company proposed to extend its operation into Lurcher's Gully. After lobbying by mountaineers and naturalists this was rejected by the planning authority. Two corries were enough of the mountain to give up to ski-ers.

The chairlift ended its useful life with the century, and is being replaced with the controversial funicular. Supporters argue that it will bring jobs and money, and that those who lack the vigour and fitness to reach the plateau under their own power deserve to share in the Cairngorm Experience.

Opponents maintain that the point of a mountain is to be difficult to get to the top of (though they use the chairlift anyway: who wants to walk up under the ugly ski-tows?). A bizarre compromise has been reached whereby those who ride the funicular won't be allowed onto the plateau. Outside the ski season, the Cairngorm Experience is to consist of a ride up in the train, an audio-visual presentation, and a chilly moment on the balcony of the Ptarmigan Restaurant.

Hillwalking is a perverse sort of sport, and I applaud this artificial way of elevating Cairngorm from its present altitude of 490ft or 148m (from the top of the chairlift) to a more realistic 2,000ft (600m). But will they make it work?

When the wind gets up the chairlifts close down; but the funicular will let us out onto the slopes on nastier days than ever before. Scottish ski-ing is different. Instead of the smooth consistent pistes of the Alps, we get: deep slush, slow as porridge, with rain falling into it; grey wrinkled ice with the skis sounding like a motorbike; tufts of heather, boulder and scree.

And then one day the wind drops, the mountains are like a wedding cake and the air's like champagne. Below, Loch Morlich makes a crazy pattern of ice and gleaming water. And the ancient trees around it are only the beginning. Down the Spey, more and more dark pines stretch into the distance: the Forest of Abernethy.

Below: Ski-ing on Cairngorm

5 STRATHSPEY AND ABERNETHY

DOWNSTREAM FROM AVIEMORE, Badenoch turns into Speyside. The river wanders across a fertile plain, now only 600ft (200m) above sea level although still 50 miles (80km) from the sea. This is a long arm of the Lowlands reaching into the hills. Here are beef and barley: the beef being the small black or brown Aberdeen Angus, and the best of the barley becoming Speyside whisky. Stone Age man settled here, and placed his chieftain's bones in the chambers of a cairn. In the Middle Ages the Strath was fortified to defend the cows and barley from the wild men of the mountains, and a strategic battle took place at Cromdale in 1661.

But Strathspey is more than mere ranch and granary. Behind the barley grows the Forest of Abernethy – 50sq miles (130sq km) of Scots pine. Though disturbed and mangled by man it has stood through thirty pine-tree lifetimes since the ice age, and is now, ever so slowly, expanding again. In another hundred years, maybe even sooner, a squirrel will once more travel branch-to-branch from Grantown to Glen Feshie.

THE DECLINE OF THE PINES

Yonder's the little glen, kingly and sweet, the haunt of the full-grown hart:
My curse on the bands of men who have robbed it of its glory.

As the ice retreated, 10,000 years ago, first the birch and then the pine moved in. Pine forest covered Highland Scotland almost to the mountaintops, with birch in the sheltered straths and oak encroaching from the warmer south.

Above: Just north of Nethy Bridge, Castle Roy is one of the oldest remaining in Scotland. It was built in 1226 by the Laird of Abernethy. Legend says that a treasure of gold is buried somewhere within the curtain wall – but beware, as the gold is infected with the plague

Left: The Spey and mountains, at the former ferry of Boat of Garten

Above left: Thuidium moss, unnoticed on the forest floor, doesn't even have an English name

Above right: Wood sorrel takes its name from the common sorrel not because they look the same (they don't) but because they have the same sharp spinach taste of oxalic acid

Below: Beard lichen on birches at Revack Estate. Lichen grows vigorously only where air and rainwater are unpolluted

Elk grazed in the clearings, and the wolf preyed on the elk. In the shadows lurked bear, lynx and wild boar.

Stone age man built forts along the riverside, and hunted under the trees. Around 1000BC started the long decline of the forest. Herdsmen and farmers of the Bronze Age were joined in the Iron Age by charcoal-burners: only charcoal gives a fire hot enough to smelt iron.

Medieval Inverness was a fur-trading port, with beaver and pine marten being trapped in the back country. The pine marten was the 'sweet mart' because its fur wasn't smelly like polecat's. It's since about AD1500 that the forest has fallen: 99 per cent of the wild pinewood has gone in the last 500 years.

A blacksmith complained of his horses wandering into Abernethy Forest, and one Cameron of Lochaber offered: 'Make me a good dirk and I'll take in hand to save you from such trouble.' The next day the whole forest was ablaze. The Cameron had disappeared, but a year later came by to claim his dirk. Other fires were started by accident, or to drive out wolves and bandits.

In 1743, three years before Culloden, Scotland's last wolf was strangled with his bare hands by a Speyside gamekeeper. But after Culloden came the clearances, and an animal that is from a pinetree point of view far more dangerous than the wolf: the sheep. Sheep straying into the forest prevent regeneration by nibbling seedlings. At the same time the former chieftains had to pay their new Hanoverian landlords. Timber was sold off for fuel to English ironmasters. Between 1780 and 1890, 300 ships were built at Spey Bay from pine floated down the river from Rothiemurchus and Abernethy. The timber demands of the Napoleonic and two World Wars also led to wide-scale logging.

The development of sporting estates increased the deer population. Too many deer means no regeneration at all in unfenced forest. At the same time Victorian egg collectors, taxidermists and gamekeepers were extinguishing the sea eagle and the osprey, the wildcat and the capercaillie.

The coming of the Forestry Commission after World War II saw a major change in the prospects of the remaining wild forest. Instead of the piecemeal destruction of the previous 500 years came a concerted effort to end the wild tree for ever. During the 1960s the Forestry Commission destroyed half of the native pinewood in its control, and damaged the rest by interplanting with alien spruce and lodgepole.

It's only in the last thirty years that the ancient forest has been recognised as a worthwhile part of the modern world. And it may have taken the Foot & Mouth year of 2001 to bring home that tourism is at least as important as farming or forestry, and that these trees are good for the pocket as well as for the soul. The first Nature Reserve was formed around the osprey nest at Loch Garten, and has now grown to cover much of what remains of Abernethy. Alien species are being removed, and the trees encouraged to regenerate up towards the natural treeline. The wildcat has been recovering since World War I drew away the gamekeepers. The pine marten is on the increase, though not, so far, the capercaillie. The osprey has returned, and there's talk of reintroducing the beaver.

OSPREYS AND OTHER BIRDS

Nothing symbolises the slow rebirth of the forest more than the return of the Scottish osprey. Shot at by gamekeepers, its nest raided by egg collectors, it became extinct in Scotland in 1899. In the 1950s a bird was spotted surveying nest sites, and in 1959 a pair settled in a dead pine alongside Loch Garten.

From the start the RSPB decided to protect the nest from, but also show it to, the public. Their observation centre is a quarter-mile (400m) from the nest, with a distant but clear view of it. Closed-circuit TV brings the nest right into the building. The Centre

itself is a simple pinewood construction, unobtrusive below the branches. With its unglazed openings and rough timber surfaces it has a semi-outdoor feel even on the inside. Over 2,000,000 people have now visited the ospreys, while the ospreys have multiplied to over 100 pairs.

The osprey is a fish-eating hawk that winters in the mangroves of the

Above: The environmental design of the RSPB Loch Garten centre even extends to the composting toilets, which use no running water. 'We supply the sawdust and you "do" the rest...'

Above: Victorian taxidermists bear much blame for the extinction of the osprey in Scotland. This example of their art is at Grantown Museum

FOREST TRAILS

Abernethy Forest has many miles of tracks for bikers. For walkers there are paths around Loch Garten, and at Dell Wood a mile east of Nethy Bridge. Gnarled and twisted 'granny pines' were the poorly shaped ones that escaped the axe. Upright stands of same-age trees may be the site of a long-ago forest fire. Pine seeds can best take root after a fire, or in bare places rubbed by boar or bear.

Below is an understorey of bilberry and cowberry, with ling heather in the clearings, and the inconspicuous forest flowers: twinflower, lady's tresses and twayblade.

Gambia and arrives in Scotland in mid-April. It dives at 100mph (160kph) to catch trout in its hooked talons. Modern trout farms, such as the one at Coylumbridge, are very good restaurants for osprey.

The zoom lens lets you see every feather, and the fierce hooked talons. A bird once it has gained a grip can even be hauled underwater and drowned: a giant pike was caught from a Highland loch with the skeleton of an osprey still hooked into its back.

Dell Wood Reserve has seventy species of breeding bird. The crested tit is one of Britain's rarest, with fewer than 1,000 pairs. It excavates its nest from a rotten stump, so can only live in wild forest. It survives on Speyside, and in 1950 a trailblazing pair reached the River Dee. Naturalists try to imagine the tiny birds flying high through the Lairig Ghru, or by an even longer route from Glen Feshie.

A favourite food is the pine-looper caterpillar. The tit eats the head and intestines (the parts most liable to go bad) then sticks the body to a twig or hides it under lichen for the winter. Experiments have shown that tits can only remember things for five minutes, but are good at looking for caterpillars in places where they might have hidden them. Even so, only one in three adults survives the winter. And when summer arrives, squirrels and pine martens take nests and young birds.

The Scottish crossbill is the only bird unique to Scotland. It is an evolutionary offshoot from the common crossbill, with a powerful cross-over beak adapted to pine cones. These it holds down with its foot, and prises apart with beak and tongue. The male is reddish-orange, the female yellowish-green. There are currently about 400 pairs.

Pine-cones take two years to ripen, and in some years there are almost none – spruce plantations are now providing backup food in bad pine-cone years. Crows and squirrels take crossbill eggs and nestlings – crows are intelligent enough to find the nests by following human birdwatchers.

Other birds to see at Dell Wood are goldcrests, waxwing and tree creeper.

CARRBRIDGE

North of Aviemore the valley expands into a strath. From Carrbridge or Dulnain Bridge you look across 10 miles (16km) of forest to the north face of the Cairngorms, still huge even at this distance. At Dulnain Bridge, ice from the distant hills has ground the bedrock into low hummocks called 'roches moutonnés'. These hummocks have their own lay-by at the junction of A95 and A938. To stand on these smoothed-off rocks and look across to the mountains is to feel through the feet the power of that ancient ice.

Carrbridge's Landmark Visitor Centre is a very large adventure playground with a lot of trees growing out of it. For the grownups there's a steam-powered sawmill, Clydesdale horses and a display showing the various injuries one can receive from a chainsaw. In the woods nearby is a very pleasant nature trail (the Ellan Wood Walk, yellow waymarks) through mixed birch and pine with ponds and sculpted benches.

Contestants from as far afield as England and Canada gather at Carrbridge for the annual World Porridge Making Championships. The winner will carry away the Golden Spurtle – a spurtle being a stick with thistle decoration used for stirring.

GRANTOWN

Grantown-on-Spey has the classic lines of a town built all at once (in 1765) and out of a single sort of stone (local granite). The buildings are well-proportioned and somewhat austere. The wide street leads up to a wide square, formerly grass but now car park. Even with the outsize enlargement of the Grant Arms Hotel, and the modern junk of street furniture and shopfront, it remains a place with very good lines. The small museum is mostly audio-visual, describing the town's beginnings.

Queen Victoria stopped at the Grant Arms in 1860. The porridge was good even then, but she didn't much enjoy the mutton-broth.

The town stands aloof on a rise above the great river. From the main street woodland paths lead down to the Spey. The wide water babbles golden under the bridge, or roars brown and foamy after the winter rains. But the great mountains that gave it birth have sunk behind the near foothills

Above: Grantown-on-Spey

Below: Carrbridge – the old packhorse bridge is hard to miss as it's right beside the modern one. The River Dulnain was noted for the Dulnain kipper – a fish caught outside the salmon season that looks like a salmon, tastes like a salmon, but can't actually be a salmon because that would be illegal

and the tops of the pines. So here we turn back south, on the old military road to Tomintoul and the whisky hills of Glenlivet. And in the end that road will lead us, between the ski-tows of the high Lecht, to Balmoral and the royal River Dee.

REAL PORRIDGE

The real thing is made from oatmeal, and bears the same relation to packetted and pre-cooked porridge oats as instant coffee does to freshly ground. The Carrbridge recipes are confidential: here's how I do it myself.

For each person:
$\frac{1}{2}$ small cup (100cc) medium oatmeal
1 small cup (200cc) cold water
small pinch salt

Soak the oatmeal overnight in the water. In the morning add the salt and bring to the boil on medium heat, stirring continually. Add up to 1 more cup (200cc) water per person, depending on how stiff you like it, and simmer on low heat for at least 5 minutes, stirring occasionally.

It is not actually un-Scottish to serve the porridge with sugar or Golden Syrup. The best combination is hot porridge with cold milk. Some dip each spoonful into a separate bowl of milk, but it's simpler to add milk to your bowl a little at a time as you go along.

Before washing a porridge saucepan, soak it in cold water for at least $\frac{1}{2}$ hour. The porridge residue can then be peeled off and fed to the hens.

The bridge of the A95 carries the date of 1931, when it was the longest concrete arch ever built: for the Spey is here almost 100yd wide. Riverside paths link this with the old bridge, a half-mile downstream

6 GLEN AVON AND THE WHISKY HILLS

LOCH AVON

From the top of the Cairngorm chairlift the ground rises in moss and boulder for 500ft (150m) to the summit of Cairngorm. After another few steps the inhabited valley drops out of sight as if it had never been, and the ground appears to roll away in boulder and moss for another 20 miles (30km). But this is not the case. After another twenty minutes of gentle descent, the plateau ends. Suddenly below is a stretch of water that is, for mountain people, one of the sacred mountain places in Scotland.

Loch Avon is not large – just 2 miles long by a quarter-mile wide. Its surface is at an altitude of 2,500ft (750m): the bottom of this lake is above the tops of most of England's hills. High though it lies, though, crag and boulder and scree rise far higher around it. Ben Macdui, Britain's second highest, is above, and Cairngorm is alongside.

At its head is Britain's most romantic bedroom, the Shelter Stone – Gaelic 'Clach Dhion'. Below the huge boulder seventeen armed men can lie together provided they don't mind walking in over a mountain to get there. Around the Stone rise the rocks: Carn Etchachan and Shelter Stone Crag and Hell's Lum.

Occasionally some come down to Loch Avon and think that with so large a lake the Lowlands must be close. And they head out the easy way, which is downstream. From Loch Avon, downstream and out is 20 miles (30km), though if you choose the left rather than the right bank of the river you will after only about three hours of bog, boulder and tussock reach a comfortable Landrover track for the rest of the way.

GLEN AVON

Two miles downstream from the loch comes a crossing of the ways, as the ancient track of the Lairig an Laoigh comes in from Glenmore to ford the River Avon. At 30 miles (48km), this cattle-drovers' route to Braemar is considerably longer than the Lairig Ghru. However it is less spectacular and more sheltered, on grass rather than stones. The name means the Pass of the Calves, as it was the gentler way preferred for the young cattle. Not that gentle, however; five men of the Morayshire Militia died here in 1804 while making their way home for the New Year.

Left: The heart of the Cairngorms: Loch Avon in midwinter splendour

QUEEN'S VIEW TOMINTOUL

The Queen's itinerary:

Day 1 (4 Sept 1860)
Start Balmoral 8.00am
Carriage to Braemar (change
horses): 9 mls
Carriage to Linn of Dee and Lower
Geldie Lodge: 10 miles
Pony to Glen Feshie: 12 miles
Lunch
Pony to ford of Spey near Loch Insh:
9 miles
Carriage to Grantown on Spey:
21 miles
Arrive Grantown 9pm (approx):
61 miles, 20 on horseback

Day 2
Start Grantown 9.50am
Carriage to Castle Grant and back:
4 miles
Carriage to Tomintoul: 12 miles
Lunch: Queen's View
Pony by Inchrory to Loch Builg:
11 miles
Carriage to Balmoral: 9 miles
Arrive Balmoral 7.30pm: 37 miles,
11 on horseback

Opposite: Ailnack Gorge

Already here the river is wide, and at times of spate or snowmelt this can be a dangerous crossing. According to legend, the Avon is Ath-Fhinn, named for the wife of Fingal who drowned in the Fords of Avon. More plausible Gaelic has it as 'Ath Fhionn', the very white. Coming straight down out of the granite, the water is clear without the peat-staining of most Scottish streams.

> *The Water of Avon, it rins sae clear*
> *Twould beguile a man o' a hunder year.*

The name is pronounced 'A'an' in both Gaelic and English – the letter V is a mistake, implausibly connecting this wildest of rivers with the gentle Warwickshire stream of Shakespeare.

Just before the river reaches civilisation at Tomintoul, a cairn high above the right bank marks where Queen Victoria stopped for lunch on the second day of her first Great Expedition from Balmoral.

The view up the Avon is typically Cairngorm: it depends for none of its effect on crag or jaggedness. Instead the great river winds back into the hills, its floodplain dotted with birchwoods below high walls of heather. Upstream the hills fold in gentle spurs, gradually rising to the skyline of Beinn Avon. That skyline is pricked with tiny tors, giving a hint of the stony wilderness far above; and on the right is a glimpse into the ravines of the Ailnack. 'A beautiful view' comments the Queen, who then goes on to scold her ghillies for their drunkenness at Grantown the night before.

Highlights of the Queen's trip were the picnic in Glen Feshie; pretending to be 'Lord Churchill and Party' and dissolving into Queenly giggles when Grant accidentally addressed Albert as 'Your Royal Highness'; and seeing two eagles at Inchrory. The Queen and Prince Albert walked short distances where the ground was too steep or too soft for the ponies. Ghillies (Brown and Grant) walked or ran alongside the ponies, so covered 31 miles (50km) on foot. In Glen Avon they 'escaped all real rain, having only a slight sprinkling now and then'.

TOMINTOUL

Tomintoul ends in 'owl' rather than 'tool'. It's an elegant village of simple, well-proportioned granite laid out along a straight main street. Like Grantown, it's a place planned and·built as a whole: in this case, by the Duke of Gordon in 1776.

Elegant, but chilly: Tomintoul lies at a height of 1,150ft (350m), and claims, along with Dalwhinnie and Braemar, to be the highest village in the Highlands. The 350m contour flows through each of the three villages – even so, the highest in Scotland is elsewhere, at Wanlockhead in Dumfriesshire, while the highest in the UK is Flash, in Derbyshire, England.

Queen Victoria found Tomintoul 'the most tumble-down poor-looking

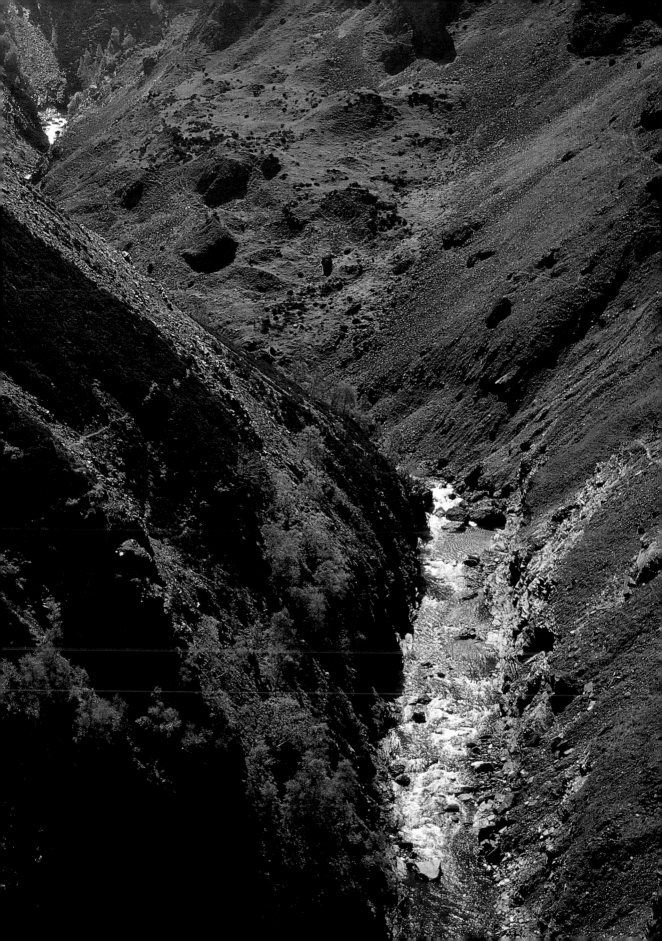

place I ever saw – a long street with three inns, miserable, dirty-looking houses and people, and a sad look of wretchedness about it. Grant told me it was the dirtiest, poorest village in the whole of the Highlands.'

Tomintoul now thrives in a gentle way on whisky tourism. Its small museum has a farmhouse kitchen and reconstructed smithy, with an exhibition on peat cutting.

THE BRAES OF GLENLIVET

Away to the east of Strath Avon is a quiet corner of pine plantations, little rivers and heather-covered hills. The Braes of Glenlivet lie in the shadow of the high Cairngorms, with less rain, less midges even, than the rest of upland Scotland.

It hasn't always been so quiet. This strategic corner is safely tucked into the hills but convenient for raiding into the cattle lands of Aberdeenshire. Here was a fort of the Wolf of Badenoch: two walls remain of Drumin Castle. A day away by the Thieves' Road is his more celebrated stronghold at Eilein Donan.

In 1594 a force of 2,000 locals in support of the Catholic Earl of Huntley routed 10,000 Highlanders under Protestant Campbell of Argyll.

Above: Tomintoul's Clock Corner

Below: Tomintoul's high, windswept position means that the planned flax and linen economy never took off. Ben Avon and Beinn a' Bhuird rise behind the village

This skirmish was part of the rebellion against James VI, the Protestant king whose Catholic mother, Mary Queen of Scots, had been executed by the English seven years before. The victory may show not so much the superior fighting qualities of the Old Religion as the home advantage. It was on the way back from this battle that the defeated army crossed not far below the summit of the Sgorans, and at the Argyll Stone paused for a first view into their home country 40 miles (60km) away. This stone is at 2,700ft (830m) – which places these Campbells among Scotland's earliest recorded mountain-climbers.

Things quietened down after the raiding days, but the Catholic faith remained strong. Through the eighteenth century, Scanlan, high above Tomnavoulin, was the only place in Scotland training men for the priest-hood. The seminary was destroyed after Culloden, but has been rebuilt.

Above: Whisky at Dalwhinnie

WHISKY

This quiet hill country with its little wooded valleys was just right for illic-it whisky. Indeed it developed a whisky economy, where every farm had its 'yowie wi' the crookit horn' – the copper condensing tube of the still. Distilling started as the barley harvest ended, and the discarded mash fed the overwintering cattle. The paths south through the Ladder Hills were originally whisky roads. Once safely away from the gaugers (excise men), whisky from the Braes was enjoyed by the wealthy and titled. 'Freedom and Whisky gang thegither' sang Robert Burns – who was an exciseman himself. And King George IV, even as his soldiers at Corgarff were attempting to destroy the stills, was demanding Glenlivet whisky by name.

In 1824, local farmer George Smith annoyed his neighbours by setting up a licensed dis-tillery at Glenlivet. To counter the understandable displeasure

Below: Glenlivet stillroom. Two small dents in this still are carefully reproduced every time the copper is replaced

of his illicit neighbours he carried two pistols in his belt at all times.

Malt whisky has a simple recipe: barley, water, yeast – but with much added mystery. When one of the copper stills has to be replaced, the accidental dents of the old one are carefully reproduced in the new in case they may have been affecting the result. Whisky straight from the still is colourless and almost flavourless. If you should ever encounter the original home-made (and illegal) product you'll find it like over-strength vodka. The colour, and much of the flavour, comes out of the oak of the second-hand sherry barrels in which the whisky lies and matures for at least seven years.

There are six whisky regions of Scotland, but the most different and distinctive are the whiskies of the Western Isles, and those of Speyside. The whisky of the West is strange and self-assertive, with flavours that Spey natives have likened to fish-crates, creosote and kelp. Speyside malts are suave and subtle. So the best way to start an understanding of malt whisky is with one from Islay and one from the Spey. And the best way to continue is in any of the hotels of Tomintoul – there are still the three as Queen Victoria found them. Behind the bar will be found a hundred fine malts; and in front of it, a number of Tomintoul's inhabitants all more than willing to share in your education.

THE DECLINE OF THE BRAES

With rich land and a good Forbes landlord, the Glenlivet Braes never suffered during the time when the Great Sheep was eating up the men. At the height of the whisky economy, over 2,500 people lived up the Livet. Today the population is lower than at any time since the Stone Age, with just six children attending the school. Tractors have replaced farm workers. Even the Glenlivet distillery is now a computerised factory (albeit a very pleasant-smelling one) and employs more people showing the place to visitors than actually making the whisky.

The best hope for the community may lie in the gentler forms of outdoor activity. While the great hills are merely a feature of the distant view, Glenlivet Estate has laid out walks and bike rides through moorland, field and forest, with occasional ruined castles and sudden views of the river.

Left: Copper pagodas of the traditional malthouse, now redundant as all Speyside distilleries use bought-in malt

7 DOWN THE DON

THE DEE AND THE DON rise at opposite corners of the Cairngorms, but eventually converge on Aberdeen in much the same way that the Brahmaputra and the Ganges converge on Dacca. Once the Avon ran on eastwards to become the head stream of the Don – and what a splendid start Loch Avon would make for Scotland's fourth-finest river. However, since the ice age its waters have been captured by a more rapidly-eroding stream from the north. Consequently the Avon turns at Inchrory sharp left into the drainage of the Spey; and ever since then the Don has had the worse of it. No great hills hang above Donside. Instead, heather slopes decline gently to a river that is, by Cairngorm standards, rather small. It's a valley of villages, pasture and plantation. Slowly through the summer the salmon work their way upstream, and this is matched, at a more modern 50mph (80kph), by Aberdonians on a Friday heading up to the ski slopes.

What does distinguish the Don is its castles. This is strategic country, remote among heather braes but within a day's raid of Perth, Aberdeen, and the rich Moray coast. Had Prince Charlie kept going after Culloden, the head of the Don would have become the central strongpoint of a mountain battleground, fascinating – if not to the inhabitants of Don and Dee – at least to military historians afterwards. The guerrilla war of the Cairngorms is one the Jacobites might very well have won.

CORGARFF

Anyone descending the Lecht Pass by daylight cannot but be struck by Corgarff. Or in the dark for that matter, as it's floodlit. Its pale, austere tower is decorated with small, random windows oddly like the twentieth-century style of Le Corbusier. Around it is a star-shaped outer wall.

The castle was of military importance in four separate centuries. The fifteenth-century tower house was a stronghold of Clan Forbes. Forbes supported the infant King James (VI of Scotland and later I of England) during the wars that followed the deposition of Mary Queen of Scots. Adam Gordon came to attack the castle, and found it defended by Margaret Forbes, the laird's wife.

Above: Corgarff Castle – the star-shaped Hanoverian fortification surrounds a much older tower house

> Gie up your house, ye fair lady,
> Gi' up your house to me,
> Or I sall burn yoursel therin
> Bot and your babies three.

LOST ON DONSIDE?

At the centre of Strathdon village is a small sign indicating 'Lost'. This may well have been the fate of militiamen from Corgarff chasing up the smugglers' paths of the Ladder Hills. However it is a genuine place above the Water of Nochty: there is now a small art gallery and sculpture garden at Lost. Further up the same glen is Duffdefiance. Here a crofter sneaked over from Glenlivet and had the house up and the lum reekin' (the chimney smoking) before the landlord Duff could notice, so gained squatter's title to the land.

The weak point of the castle was its sewage system. The besiegers removed the 'grund-wa' stane' that blocked the bottom of the latrine chute, and introduced fire into the castle. Lady Forbes, the babies, and twenty-two of her followers were burned.

The castle was burned again in 1689 by the Jacobites during the rebellion against William of Orange. It was burned in 1716 by both Jacobite and Government forces. 'One can only hope,' remarks Hamish MacInnes in his 1988 guidebook, 'that the present occupiers have it insured.'

After the failure of the 1745 rebellion, Corgarff and Braemar were re-fortified, and linked into the system of military roads. The star-shaped outer wall represents this Hanoverian stage of military architecture: it's designed for defence with the musket. The castle continued until 1831 as a patrol post against whisky smugglers.

Eight miles (13km) down-valley, the village of Strathdon has the earth hill of an earlier motte and bailey. Strathdon is important today as the site of Scotland's second-largest Highland games, the Lonach Gathering. The Glasgow comedian Billy Connolly, who played Queen Victoria's devoted servant John Brown in the film *Mrs Brown*, occupies a pinkish-coloured castle near the village. Connolly's friend the American actor Robin Williams earned the respect of the locals by competing in the hill race at the gathering, although finishing an undistinguished second-from-last.

GLENBUCHAT

Further down the Don is a castle that hasn't been burned down even once, and retains its roof and all twelve walls. Glenbuchat is a fine example of the 'Z-shaped' castle: rectangular with a huge tower on two opposite corners. John Gordon, known as Old Glenbucket, was a staunch supporter of the Earl of Mar in the rebellion of 1715: so much so that George II had bad dreams about him. In the King's Hanoverian English: 'De gread Glenbogged is goming.'

KILDRUMMY

Friends of Historic Scotland can here recoup a quarter of their year's subscription in one day, as all three Donside castles are in its care. Kildrummy is the largest of the three and the oldest, built in the prosperous 1240s as a showpiece residence for the Earl of Mar.

In 1306, during the Scottish War of Independence, the castle was held by Neil Bruce, brother of the recently-crowned King Robert; the King's female family sheltered there as well. The English under Edward Prince of Wales set a siege which is celebrated in the epic poem *The Bruce* by John Barbour. They bribed the castle blacksmith, one Osborne, who set fire to the grain being stored in the great hall, and burnt down the castle. It's said that

Below: Restored stonework at Kildrummy shows off the colours of the local granite

Edward paid the traitor Osborne his promised gold by pouring it, molten, down his throat.

Neil Bruce was executed at Berwick. The Queen and Princess had fled the castle but were soon captured. Bruce's sister Mary and his elderly supporter Isabel Countess of Buchan were placed in open cages hung from the walls of Berwick and Roxburgh Castles – presumably in the hope that Bruce would attempt a rescue. Twelve-year-old Princess Margery was imprisoned at the Tower of London. Seven years later the Queen and Princess were exchanged against English prisoners taken at Bannockburn.

The castle remained the noble residence of the Earls of Mar right up to 1715. The rebellion of that year was planned within its walls. 'Bobbing John' then rode upstream to Corgarff to gather his forces. Castle-chasing has carried us far down the Don. We shall now follow Bobbing John across into Deeside; though not, perhaps, going so far as to raise the standard of rebellion at the Invercauld Hotel in Braemar. After all, Scotland now has limited self-rule – and even a prince called Charlie.

Below: Kildrummy Castle, scene of three sieges and a conspiracy

8 UPPER DEESIDE: BRAERIACH TO BRAEMAR

NO BRITISH RIVER has a finer start in the world than the Dee. High on the side of Braeriach, several powerful springs leap out of the mountainside. At 4,000ft (1,220m) this is the third-highest flowing water in the country; only the March Burn and the Tailor Burn on Ben Macdui rise higher.

The river emerges into the famous pass of the Lairig Ghru. Already it has reached a dangerous size: a footbridge has been built by Aberdeen's Engineering Department using the same structure (but smaller) as Sydney Harbour Bridge. This leads to Corrour, a hut built for the watchers who kept track of deer movements. It is now a refuge maintained by the Mountain Bothies Association.

BOTHIES OR NOT?

Open bothies like Corrour are a romantic refuge among the mountains. Shut out the rain and most of the midges, and exchange whisky and conversation with whatever stranger fate has brought in off the mountain. However, such shelters do make the mountains smaller and more accessible.

A hut that used to stand near the top of the Lairig was removed ten years ago. The building of the car park at Coire Cas meant that the top of the pass was no longer remote enough to justify its existence. Another hut on the plateau near Cairngorm was demolished after Scotland's worst ever mountain accident. A party of young people and teachers relying on its shelter failed to find it under the snow.

The ground around Corrour has suffered from litter, and worse, left by walkers. Mar Lodge Estate has considered the removal of this historic bothy, as well as the elegant footbridge leading to it. Heroic clean-up efforts by the volunteers of the MBA mean that the hut is still permitted to exist for the time being.

Behind the bothy rise the gleaming granite slabs of Bod an Deamhain. 'And what does that mean?' asked Queen Victoria, passing below on her pony. Quick-witted, the ghillie replied, 'The Devil's Point, Ma'am.' Gaelic is a curiously plain-speaking language: the name actually means the Devil's Penis.

Right: The wide floodplain of the Dee below Mar Lodge

Above: The Devil's Point and Cairn Toul look over the beginning of the Dee. Just 5 miles (8km) down from the Wells of Dee the river is already large enough to cause drownings

Opposite: Linn of Dee. The bridge was opened by Queen Victoria in 1857 with pipers, a triumphal arch and whisky. As the Queen herself points out, the view of the Linn is very fine from it

THE GAELIC-SPEAKING GHOST

Before the coming of the deer, this empty valley was busy with people and livestock. Here at a house called Dabrach lived Peter Grant who fought at Culloden. 'Oh lat's throw awa' thae fushionless things o' guns, ere we get doon upon the smatchets wi' our swords!' he cried in frustration during that battle, so badly generalled on the Jacobite side. He was captured and led away to Carlisle jail but managed to escape.

In 1822 this campaigner was 108 years old. King George IV granted him a pension and came to shake his hand. 'You are the oldest of my friends.'

"Naa, naa, yer Majesty," Aald Dabrach replied. 'I am yer aaldest enemy!' At his funeral two years later the pipes played 'Wha Widna Fecht for Charlie'.

During Dabrach's absence his house was a redcoat garrison – this is an important junction of routes to Speyside, Atholl and Dee. In 1749 a Sergeant Davis disappeared when out hunting in the heather. At the subsequent murder trial, the principal witness was the victim's ghost...

Donald Farquharson testified on the spirit's behalf, saying that it had appeared to him to insist that he should bury its bones. After Farquharson had found the bones at the place described, the spirit went

THE EARL'S PUNCH

John Grant, in Legends of the Braes of Mar, *has recorded the (rather vague) recipe:*

*Whisky: some ankers
    (8 gallon casks)
Boiling water: some gallons
Honey: some hundredweights*

Pour together and drink.

Below: On this ledge in the gorge of the Water of Ey, the Black Colonel took refuge after the burning of his castle. He is even said to have shared this uncomfortable and rather dangerous bed with Annie Bhan

on to name its murderers as Duncan Clerk and Alexander MacDonald.

Farquharson was the servant of Isobel MacHardie, and she, sleeping at the other end of the shieling, also saw the spirit. But she drew the blankets over her head and heard nothing of what passed – for the ghost had appeared without any clothes on.

When asked how the ghost had spoken to him, Farquharson replied 'in the Irish language' – that is, in Gaelic. This was finally too much for the Jury, who unanimously found the accused not guilty.

LINN OF DEE

Since its source 16 miles away at an altitude of almost 4,000ft the Dee has dropped to 1,200ft (in 25km it's dropped from 1,200m to 350m). This is well below the natural tree-line, but the area is heavily grazed by deer and it is only now that the river comes among pines.

Here at the highest point of the public road is a fine stone bridge in the Baronial style. 'Linn' is a gorge pool, as also at Linn of Muick. Duncan Grey, the frustrated lover in Burns' poem, 'spak o' lowpin in a Linn' – threatened to end his miseries by jumping into one. A burn named after Duncan Grey runs into the Dee just below White Bridge. With the pines above, the black waters of the linn below and car parks nearby, this is a popular picnic spot as well as the launch-point for expeditions to Macdui, Cairn Toul and the Lairig Ghru.

The road doubles back downstream on the northern side, to end at the Linn of Quoich. Here is another attractive scene of rock, water, pine and car park. A large pot hole in the riverbed is visible when the river isn't too full. It is the Earl of Mar's Punch Bowl, supposedly filled for the refreshment of his followers after a great deer-hunt through the forests of Glen Clunie.

THE BLACK COLONEL OF INVEREY

John Farquharson, the Black Colonel, used to have his castle at Inverey. In its great hall, he would summon his servant by firing his pistol at a great shield hanging on the wall.

Once when trapped between two troops of dragoons in the narrow Pass of Ballater, he rode his black mare straight up the steep and bouldery slope on the northern side. After Killiecrankie (1689), government troops came to burn down his castle; he is supposed to have made his escape stark naked while his mistress Annie Bhan (fair-haired Annie) hurled the first of the soldiers down the castle steps with 'Cabh an donus thu' – 'May the Devil take you'.

Even after death he was a formidable figure. He'd arranged to be buried at Inverey alongside Annie Bhan; but his family felt it more respectable to inter him at Braemar. Three times his bones dug themselves up of their own accord before the family gave way to his wishes.

MAR LODGE

This lies on the north side of the Dee, its rectangle providing a focus-point for a view that's otherwise composed of broad curves of hill and river. There's no call to examine it closer – Mar Lodge has twice burnt down, each time rebuilt in greater baronial splendour, with an excessive use of creosoted pine trees. Unusually (for Deeside), the earlier Mar Lodges were burnt by accident rather than by enemies. The use as decorative features of kilted Highlanders bearing flaming torches may be to blame here; and the one thing to be said in favour of creosoted pine trunks is that they do go up nicely. 'Save the antlers!' cried the Duke of Fife – but alas, the twenty-seven antlers along the gable end were already alight. After a third fire in 1991 came a radical break from tradition. Instead of rebuilding the Lodge even worse than before, they carefully rebuilt it just the same.

The Earls of Fife, whose family name is Duff, became the Dukes of Fife when one of them married the Princess Alice. 'A splendid match,' remarked her mother Queen Victoria, 'he is immensely rich.'

After passing through various hands the estate was obtained in 1995 by the National Trust for Scotland. For their £5,500,000 they got around half of the Cairngorms: 117sq miles (300sq km) of heather and granite, including fifteen Munro summits. Plus a whole lot of problems – the forest in particular is in very poor shape after 120 years of overgrazing by deer; intrusive Landrover tracks run into the heart of the hills; and monster footpaths scar the most popular routes. It took almost five years to work out the combination of man and machine for the removal of a vehicle track from the fragile ground high on the plateau of Beinn a' Bhuird. Boulders must be replaced lichen side up!

WALK: GLEN EY TO COLONEL'S BED

3 miles (5km) return: track, path and short scramble.

From Inverey take the track past the Duke of Fife's shooting lodge, then the lower (right-hand) of two tracks up-valley. This crosses the river at Drochaid an Leum, the Bridge of the Leap, where the naked Colonel sprang across before viewing the destruction of the castle from Craig a' Chait (Cat Crag) opposite. To right of Cat Crag appears Derry Cairngorm, a perfect cone from this viewpoint.

After 1 mile (1.5km), a small sign 'Col Bed' indicates the path down to the gorge. A small but obvious path scrambles down to the water itself. From here the Bed can be seen just downstream. A recent rockfall lies across the ledge: I crossed it myself but cannot guarantee its stability.

Left: Mar Lodge is only open to the public on two or three days a year – which is a shame, as the ballroom is decorated with 2,435 stag's heads. The surrounding estate is open hill ground, available to all

Pages 80–1: Braemar at daybreak from the slopes of Morrone

Walk: Morrone Birkwood

2 miles (3km) on paths, sometimes wet.

From the junction at the west end of the village, walk or drive up Chapel Brae to a car park at the duck pond. Follow a track to right of the pond, forking left at a signpost, going through a deer fence, and at once turning left at a blue-topped waymark. Above Tomintoul House fork left to a viewpoint indicator.

Now a wide path contours to the right, through ground of heather, juniper, bilberry and downy birch. There are views across the reserve to Deeside and the high peaks beyond. Where the path reaches a plantation, with a gate ahead, a waymark indicates a smaller path turning back to the right. This path divides confusingly, so keep the wooded hump of Creag Choinnich ahead. Eventually the various paths rejoin, to lead back to the duck pond.

Braemar

The Clunie Water divides the estates of Mar and Invercauld, and also the village of Braemar. Each half-village has its own name. On the western side is Auchendryne; across the river is Castleton. Each has its own inn: the Fife Arms, and the Invercauld Arms. And when the Duke of Fife drove through Castleton and noticed they were building a new hall for Queen Victoria's Jubilee, he went back to his own side of the river and built a new hall there as well. The Castleton Jubilee Hall is now the Invercauld Galleries; the wooden Jubilee Hall at Invercauld stands on the road towards Linn of Dee.

Braemar is at the junction of valleys running east, west and south. It has been a strongpoint since the time of Kenneth MacAlpin, first king of the combined Picts and Scots. The eleventh-century King Malcom Canmore held contests here to select swordsmen for his army and runners for his messenger service. Two MacGregor lads from Ballochbuie entered the race up Creag Choinnich (the wooded hill above Castleton). Just after the race had started the third brother panted onto the field, and overtook all the other runners. His eldest brother grabbed him to hold him back but he slipped out of his kilt and took the lead. His winning time is given as just three minutes.

The more formal Braemar gathering started in 1826, with contests in piping, dancing, and the traditional sports of shot and caber. Queen Victoria was pleased when one of her own ghillies won the Creag Choinnich race, even though with the passing of the heroic age the winning time had slowed to 6½ minutes. 'After the race the winner spit blood and has never been so well since. The running up the hill has consequently been discontinued.' However, the modern games include a race to the highest visible point (the five cairns) on Morrone, with winning times of about

twenty-five minutes. They take place on the first Saturday in September.

The present-day path up Creag Choinnich starts at a gate uphill from the church where there is a signpost. Those prepared to take more than six minutes over the ascent can enjoy a very fine view over the village into Upper Deeside, with the tors of Beinn Avon along the skyline.

Malcom's castle was Kindrochit, 300yd upstream from the bridge over the Clunie that joins the two villages. The visible remains are of a later castle of the fourteenth century. It's said that this castle was destroyed by gunfire as a way of culling the occupants, who were infected with the 'gatar mor' or plague.

The Invercauld Arms lies on the spot where the Earl of Mar (known as Bobbing John) raised the standard for the Old Pretender in 1715. As punishment for his leading role in the rebellion, his tenants suffered eviction and dispossession nearly a hundred years before the rest of the Highlands. In a house opposite the hotel, Robert Louis Stevenson wrote part of *Treasure Island*. However, his Highland classic *Kidnapped* took his heroes down the western side of Scotland and sadly lacks a Cairngorm chapter.

Various colour-coded walks have been laid out around Braemar, including the one up Creag Choinnich. The finest of them is through the Morrone Birkwood, a nature reserve just above the village.

WALK: MORRONE

7 miles (11km) on hill path, track and road.

From the viewpoint above the Braemar duck pond (Morrone Birkwood walk) a path continues to the summit of Morrone. The path is fairly steep and wet, and stout footwear is recommended. The ascent takes around two hours, with steadily improving views.

At the summit are a large cairn, radio mast and the hut erected by the Mountain Rescue team. A descent of the radio access track offers new views along Loch Callater to the White Mount. This route takes you down to Glen Clunie, for a half-hour stroll down the road back into the village.

Left: On the summit of Morrone lived the old witch Cailleach Bheathrach, who fed herself by milking the hinds of the forest. The remains of her dwelling have been incorporated into this Nature Reserve signboard

Above: Braemar Castle, just outside the village towards Balmoral, was the 1628 replacement for Kindrochit. It was burnt down by the Black Colonel of Inverie. After the 1745 Rising it was burnt again, by the Government.

The restored castle is open to the public from Easter to October (though anyone carrying matches and a can of petrol will be looked on with grave suspicion). Among its less attractive attractions are the Old Laird's Pit: a former prison below the floor dating from when the Earl of Mar had powers of imprisonment and execution over his tenants. The castle also shows a piece of Bonnie Prince Charlie's plaid, and the world's largest Cairngorm – a 52lb (24kg) monster.

9 LOWER DEESIDE: BALMORAL AND BALLATER

The glen along which the Dee winds, with beautiful wooded hills, reminded us very much of the Thuringerwald. The scenery is wild, and yet not desolate; and everything looks much more prosperous and cultivated than at Laggan.

Queen Victoria

Below Braemar the Dee flows out of the granite into a new sort of country. The rock is now the hard schist of the main Highland block, with a touch of the exotic in the limestone of Creag Choinnich. Instead of huge, gently-sloping and distant mountains, the river runs between small craggy hills that reminded Queen Victoria of Thuringia – the romantic part of Germany that was birthplace of Prince Albert.

Victoria and Albert arrived in this exotic back country of their kingdom with an unquenchable enthusiasm and determination to have fun. Before supper she would be called out to admire by the light of flaring torches the deer carcasses flopped across the doorstep like dead mice left by some giant cat. Then they would listen to the bagpipes: it's been calculated that no one has listened to quite so much bagpipe music as Prince Albert did. 'The bagpipes always played about breakfast time, again during the morning, at luncheon, and also whenever we went in and out, again before dinner, and during most of dinnertime. We both have become quite fond of the bagpipes.'

Prince Albert was a poor shot – once when he did manage to hit a stag it wasn't actually the one he'd been aiming at. This never deterred him from crawling off into the heather after any passing grouse or deer. His combination of being no good at it but immensely enthusiastic embodies an attitude to sport that we now think of as peculiarly British.

Her descendants still enjoy the so-called 'Royal Sports' in pursuit of the local wildlife. The present Queen Mother was photographed in a remarkably scruffy old hat fishing the River Dee.

SALMON

Two hundred years ago, the rivers were so full of salmon that people claimed to walk from bank to bank treading on their backs. In a single year, 56,000 fish were taken in nets or fish-traps in just three pools of the Don. In 1850 Victoria and Albert took part in salmon 'leistering' in the Spey. The leister was the traditional barbed and three-pointed fish spear. 'They all went into the river, poking about under all the stones to bring fish up to where men stood with the net. It had a very pretty effect; about 100 men wading through the river, some in kilts with poles and spears, all very much excited.' Eight salmon were caught and the Queen made a lively sketch.

Salmon was smoked on chimney-bars above the peat fires, and was a valuable food to store through the winter. Today, an angler will pay thousands of pounds for a week on one of these prime rivers and be happy to catch even two or three fish. The catch for the whole of the River Dee in 1999 was 2,230, all of which were put back alive into the river. The huge decline in salmon numbers has been blamed on drift-netting around Iceland, the increase in North Sea seals since they became a protected species, and bag-netting at river mouths. Angling associations have bought up and discontinued all netting at the mouth of the Dee, and salmon stocks are recovering.

In 1930 a forestry student called Frank Harper tried a different sort of sport. In imitation of the loggers of previous centuries, he floated a raft of treetrunks down the Dee to raise £50 for the University's Charities Week. The trip from Banchory to Aberdeen took him just two hours.

Not nearly so well-paid were the men of the previous century who rode the logs down the Spey and the Dee. In Scotland the logs were tied together into rafts rather than piling down the river loose in the Canadian fashion. This was to protect the many bridges on the way downstream. The men who rode the rafts were always wet, and sometimes crushed to death as they cleared log-jams or 'cairns' with crowbars or explosives. Seton Gordon describes their bothy at Aviemore: 'The floaters after a hard day on the river lay down on beds of heather in their wet clothes, each man's feet to the fire, each man's plaid round his chest, a circle of wearied bodies half stupefied by whisky, enveloped in a cloud of steam and smoke, and sleeping soundly till morning.'

In the 1970s, canoeists cited the Spey floaters to establish the public right to navigate, irrespective of who owned the banks on either side or the fishing underneath.

Below: Balmoral Castle

BALMORAL

In September 1848, the year when half Europe was in revolution and lesser monarchs were trembling on their thrones, Victoria and Albert arrived on Deeside to take possession of 'a pretty little castle in the old Scottish style... there is a nice little hall, and a billiard-room.'

Within two years this castle had been cleared away for a more suitably-sized one, with three times the turrets and a better view up the river. Prince Albert designed it himself, with some help from Mr William Smith of Aberdeen.

What is it that makes Balmoral Castle so unsatisfactory? There's the cold greyish beige of its granite, though even this is less ugly than the concrete of the Hilton Hotel at Aviemore. But basically it's the style called Scottish Baronial that takes the traditional castle and gets it wrong. The clean lines and proper proportions of Corgarff, or the more modern Braemar Castle – or Castle Grant, which to Queen Victoria looked like a factory – are spoilt in various ways to make them more romantic. Pepperpot turrets were originally sentry-boxes; but the basic structure is in origin a privy, overhanging for a form of external drainage without any drains. The Scottish Baronial makes them into mere decorative effects, but decoration that is as heavy and ponderous as the jokes in a Gilbert and Sullivan opera.

The rounded corners of Braemar Castle are designed to be hard to knock out with pickaxe or cannonball. It'd be interesting – outside the Royal months of August and September of course, we're talking architectural experiment not high treason here – to attack Balmoral with cannon and see how long it would take to fall down...

The interior design was also by Albert. Lord Clarendon objected to the use of tartan for both floors and wallpaper, but even worse was the 'abundance of thistles; they would rejoice the heart of a donkey if they happened to look like his favourite repast – which they don't'.

The castle does have an interesting selection of small outbuildings and statues. There is the circular Game Larder, decorated with antlers. There is a somewhat disgruntled wild boar, and Prince Albert on a pile of boulders. Hubert, patron saint of hunters, kneels before a stag in a niche of the west wall.

Those interested in Queen Victoria's faithful servant John Brown will have to hunt for him in the woods. The Queen's son, Edward VII, destroyed pictures and mementos of Brown and moved his statue to its present inconspicuous position above the dairy. Even in the Queen's lifetime her relationship with Brown was a subject of scandal, and she was referred to mockingly as Mrs Brown. This is also the name of the recent film about them starring Judi Dench and Billy Connolly.

Brown's statue shows him wearing a remarkably hairy sporran, as well as the Devoted Service Medal, which was invented specially for him by the

Above: To find the statue of John Brown, follow the Mountain View walk (red waymarks) uphill for 200yd. Where this bends right, a blue arrow indicates a broad path running downhill on the left (southeast). The statue is reached after 400yd.

Below left: John Brown's lucky threepenny piece

Below right: Balmoral sentry box

Opposite: Above Invercauld Bridge an old whisky-smugglers' path leads uphill under the ancient pines of Ballochbuie. It passes the waterfalls of the Garbh-allt (rough stream), where various scenic bridges have been built and fallen down over the last 150 years

Queen and never awarded to anyone else. Beside it hangs his lucky three-penny, which, like every coin of the realm, carries the Queen's picture. The sculptor Boehm has even shown what's under the kilt... It ought to be nothing at all; but to avoid any chance of a royal flush Brown wore a pair of short trews. John Brown was born in 1826, so was in his thirties, and seven years younger than the Queen, at the time of her pony-treks.

Crathie Church is a squat granite box with a pointed tower. It's an unattractive building, celebrated only as the place where Victoria and her descendants have attended Sunday worship. John Brown is buried here: he died of erisypelas aggravated by whisky. After visiting his grave, you can cross the river to taste the whisky itself at the Royal Lochnagar Distillery.

WHITE MOUNTH

The main Cairngorms are far upstream. The mountain that dominates Balmoral is Lochnagar, high point of the White Mounth.

The White Mounth can be considered as Cairngorms Lite: the same granite crag and boulder, the same pinewood and waterfall, but in a handier package. Along the northern wall, crumbling rocks rise in not twenty but just two loch-bottomed corries. The one under Lochnagar offers first-rate rock and ice climbs. Behind the summit the plateau extends for just 8 miles (12km), to Caenlochan and Glen Clova. This is lower than the Cairngorm plateau, and instead of stones and occasional azaleas has wide rolling grassland. It's slightly unexciting ground, with the compensation that a tour of its giant high-altitude meadow can net the walker ten or more Munro summits.

The true Cairngorms have Loch Avon. The White Mounth has the Dubhloch, which is smaller but every bit as spectacular, and a lot less trouble to get to. The path from Glas-allt-Shiel was widened for Queen Victoria and her pony, so is the first ever built specifically for hillwalking. And lying along the bottom of all this is the area's greatest lake. Loch Muick lies below high mountainsides, fringed with birch and rowan, surrounded by waterfalls.

So it's unsurprising that every line drawn round the prospective Cairngorms National Park has expanded to snatch the White Mounth and Lochnagar.

DARK LOCHNAGAR

At the farm of Ballaterach, 4 miles (6km) downstream from Ballater, an 'ill-tricket nickum fae Aberdeen, Geordie Byron' spent his boyhood holidays: falling in love with the farmer's daughter sweet Mary Robinson, making a nuisance of himself in the carpenter's workshop, and climbing up Morven. In 1803, at the age of fifteen, he made his ascent of Lochnagar.

His path was from Invercauld, apparently by the Stuic, a demanding route for a lame man (Byron suffered from club foot). His guide writes: 'His

WALK: ROUND LOCH MUICK

*7½ miles (12km) on tracks
and paths.*

*From Spittal car park a sandy track
runs to the loch and along its south
side. Where it strikes away uphill a
path continues around the lochside.
This is quite bouldery and rough,
but has views to Queen Victoria's
lochside house and the waterfalls of
Allt an Dubh-loch.*

*After the loch head a stalkers'
path runs up left to the Dubh Loch
– a worthwhile side trip. The main
path continues ahead to the
plantation at Glas-allt Shiel. Here a
sign indicates a left fork to pass up
the plantation edge and circle above
the house before dropping to its
driveway track.*

*The track runs past a boat
house to the cottages at Allt na
Giubhsaich, which was the royal
refuge before the building of
Glas-allt Shiel. A track on the
right returns to the car park.*

Lordship rested often and looked at the scenery. He was very quiet and did
not often speak to me. When we began to climb the crags of Loch nan Eun
I thought he would not be able to scramble up, but he would not have any
help from me. When we got to the top he sat a long time on the edge of the
rocks, looking about him, but seldom asked me any question.'

But Byron had plenty to say about Lochnagar afterwards.

*England thy beauties are tame and domestic
To one who has roved o'er the mountains afar;
Oh for the crags that are wild and majestic,
The steep frowning glories of dark Lochnagar!*

Queen Victoria made her expedition by an easier route on 16 September
1848, just days after arriving at Deeside for the very first time. Thus she
became the first Royal Munro-bagger since Bonnie Prince Charlie (Sgurr
nan Coireachain 1746). Her ascent from Ballochbuie, mostly on pony,
took four hours: like Byron and many since, she stopped for a picnic
looking down at Loch nan Eun. For her Lochnagar was always 'the jewel
of all the mountains here'. Five generations later, the present Prince
Charles has expressed his affection for the hill in his book for children
The Old Man of Lochnagar.

ABERGELDIE AND THE WITCHES' HILL

Three miles (5km) downstream from Braemar is a smaller and older castle
that makes an interesting contrast. Abergeldie, built around 1550, is a pink-
coloured tower with small windows and just one turret. It is not open to the
public, but can be seen across the river from the main Deeside road; or, on
the south side of the river, from the Witches' Hill above it, Creag nam Ban.

Witches were burned on the summit of Creag nam Ban, including a
maid from the castle below called Kitty Rankine. The future King Edward
VIII met what he believed to be her ghost in the castle's little tower. (It's said
that every single one of Scotland's 1,000 castles is haunted.) Earlier, a witch
and warlock were imprisoned in the castle but the witch escaped in the
form of a hare. The warlock offered to recapture her in return for his own
freedom. He turned himself into a greyhound and gave chase. The witch
changed into a mouse and slipped between the stones, but the warlock
became a weasel and captured her.

The Birks (birch trees) of Abergeldie were celebrated in a local song
'Bonnie lassie, will ye gae, To the Birks o' Abergeldie', which Rabbie Burns
rewrote and relocated to the 'Birks o' Aberfeldy'. These birches were famous
in wine as well as in song: the drink prepared from the birch sap was selling in 1845 for a shilling a bottle, and reported to be better than the best
champagne.

A less appetising regional delicacy was prepared in times of scarcity by gathering slugs and salting them down in jars. The resulting paste could be cut into slices and fried. It sounds just the thing for adventurous eaters who think haggis is old hat.

The ground alongside the Dee is rich farmland, so there's no profit in turning it over to sheep. Thus the sizeable community that stood opposite Abergeldie Castle was not a victim of the Clearances but simply dwindled over the following century. The last of the old life survived just long enough to be captured by the tape-recorders of the twentieth century. 'The smell of the hills and the air was so wonderful, at night the whole valley was filled with the sound of the bagpipes.' The women gathered lichen off the field walls to make dye for cloth, and at the old house of Lebhall the turf lay so thick on the roof that ferrets were sent up after the rabbits in it.

Now the Dee reaches a triple valley point. From the north Glen Gairn runs down from the high pass that leads across to Donside and Tomintoul. From the south arrives Glen Muick, where the area's largest and finest loch lies along the flank of Lochnagar. Queen Victoria built herself a holiday cottage here: for today's visitor there is a small information centre and rather large car park at Spittal of Glenmuick.

Four miles (6km) down the glen are large waterfalls at Linn of Muick, though these lack convenient car parking. Near the foot of the glen is Birkhall, which is the Queen Mother's Deeside residence. Here she taught Prince Charles the rudiments of fly-fishing. And at the foot of the river, and the junction of the glens, is the pale and elegant town of Ballater.

BALLATER

Like Grantown and Tomintoul, Ballater is a planned town. It was put up in 1770 to exploit the healing waters of a spring at Pannanich.

> *I've seen the sick to health return*
> *I've seen the sad forget to mourn*
> *I've seen the lame their crutches burn*
> *And loup and fling at Pannanich.*
>
> *I've seen the auld seem young and frisky*
> *Without the aid of ale or whisky*
> *I've seen the dullest hearts grow brisky*
> *At blithesome, healthful Pannanich.*
> James Ogilvy, 1800s

The springs and inn of Pannanich are to south of the Dee on the B979, 2 miles (3km) east of the town. In 1796 the young Byron was cured of scarlet fever by a course of the healing waters and goat's milk. But for those who feel they might become even more young and frisky with the aid of ale or whisky, not to mention a bite to eat, Ballater is today particularly

Top: Abergeldie Castle, where the wine is birch-sap, the women are witches, and the song is 'The Birks o' Abergeldie'

Above: Loch Muick. Muick is pigs: not a pretty name, as Queen Victoria pointed out, but a pretty place

Opposite: Watch out for Deeside's red squirrels

91

WALK: CRAIGENDARROCH
2 miles (3km) on steep paths.

From the centre of Ballater head out on the A93 towards Braemar for 200yd. Opposite the Old Kirk Hotel a street on the right is Craigendarroch Walk. A path on the left leads onto the hill.

After 50yd turn sharply back left at a sign 'To Top'. The path climbs in steep zig-zags past a bench, then slants to left through oaks. After ¼ mile (400m) a steep path climbing to the right is signed 'To Top'. As you ascend you pass through the ecological strata, from oakwood through birches to the bare rock and pines at the summit cairn.

A small path runs on (northeast) past the highest point of the hill, then joins a larger one to slant down to the right and return to the street called Craigendarroch Walk.

well-provided: from triple-rosette restaurants to what's generally considered one of the best chippies in all Scotland.

The small hill of Craigendarroch, the Crag of the Oaks, rises out of the town. It has, as the name suggests, oakwoods at the bottom, and ice-scraped granite at the top with a fine Dee view. Down the glen the eye passes over the pinewoods of Cambus o' May to the open country around Dinnet and the beginning of the coastal lowlands. Upstream the valley winds between ever tighter shoulders of the hill, some wooded, some bare heather. High on the left rise the cliffs of Lochnagar.

In our circuit of Speyside, the Don and the Dee we have seen all that can be seen through car windows, or even in the oft-advised stout shoes. For the final chapter we follow the eagle and the experienced hillwalker upwards onto the high plateau.

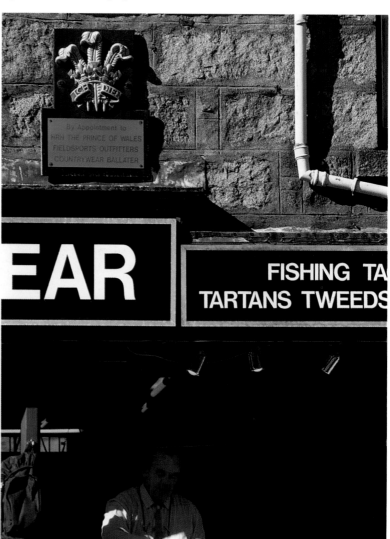

Right: Prince Charles' outdoor gear shop. Royal coats of arms decorate many Ballater shops

Opposite: This is the 'Fourth Road Bridge': three previous bridges at Ballater (two stone, one wooden) have been carried away by the River Dee

10 THE MOUNTAIN GROUND

AND FINALLY WE COME to the world above the World. For the eagle it takes about thirty seconds, for the human walker about three hours, to pass from the great pines, up through the heather moorland, onto the gravel and boulder. The high plateau stretches for 20 miles (30km), from the head of the Don to lovely glen of Feshie. Apart from the two deep glacier-slashes of the Lairig Ghru and the Lairig an Laoigh it's above 3,000ft (900m) the whole way.

BEN AVON AND BEINN A' BHUIRD

The eastern section of the range consists of two sprawling hills. Ben Avon is an amoeboid lump, distinguished by the variety of its granite tors. One of them, Leabaidh an Daimh Buidhe, is the actual summit of the mountain: this makes Ben Avon the hardest of the Cairngorms as, on top of the long walk in from any direction and the climb to nearly 4,000ft (1,200m), it requires a small amount of rock-climbing.

From the west Beinn a' Bhuird is as flat and featureless as its name, Table Hill, suggests. This impression is, as elsewhere in the range, quite one-sided. To the east the plateau ends abruptly in a sudden precipice, at the foot of which quite large lakes twinkle derisively. And in the north, overlooking Glen Avon, is an even huger hole called the Slochd Mor. The crags here include the famous Mitre Ridge, first climbed by two separate parties on two separate routes on one July day of 1933.

On this high ground, the weather is bad and the soils are poor. Granite breaks down into a thin sand that's acidic and low in nutrients. Rain and snowmelt, it drains away through the gravel; this, combined with the drying effect of wind, means that plantlife has difficulty retaining moisture.

Above: Tormentil plant gains a roothold in a crystalline chunk of granite
Below: Loch Avon – at nearly 3,000ft above sea level, this loch is higher than most of Britain's summits

SNOW BUNTING

The snow bunting is not unlike a sparrow in shape and behaviour, but slightly larger: pale biscuitty colour above, white below. It can be seen during the ski season picking up crumbs around the Shieling snack bar. The bird appears less sparrow-like when looking for seedheads among the snow, and a cheering sight is a flock of them in bobbing flight across the dim winter plateau.

The birds head north for the more bracing climate of the Arctic summer, so are seen mainly between October and April, though a few pairs remain in the Cairngorms to breed.

Grass does not thrive, and instead we see low-growing shrubs like bearberry and crowberry. A true tree, the least willow grows to a height of a few centimetres at best. The pink thrift flowers here, high above its normal seaside habitat. In Gaelic it's cluasag mhuire, the Virgin Mary's pillow. Across the stonefields nothing grows but the grey-green lumps of woolly hair moss, but where a stream meanders across the plateau the ground is bright with red-to-green tones of sphagnum moss.

PTARMIGAN

The ptarmigan is one of only two birds whose common English name is in Gaelic. Gaelic is a language with rational spelling, so the original 'tarmachan' lacks that pointless letter P.

The ptarmigan is a game bird, though it's been said that the only sporting way to hunt it is to walk up to it with a revolver: it sits tight and relies on its excellent camouflage, speckled grey in summer, white in winter. It looks like a small grey hen with furry feet. The sharp-eyed hillwalker will often get a very close sighting before the bird walks briskly off around a boulder.

The sharp-eyed motorist, however, won't see it at all. It's a true bird of the mountains, feeding on crowberry, bearberry and heather around the 900m contour. At the same time the bird itself is food for eagles and foxes. As the snow melts, you'll hear its so-called 'song', a mixture of cackles and belches, as the cock bird asserts its territory.

The bird adapts to human presence, nesting close to paths and ski-slopes. However, many young birds die by flying into ski-tow wires in mist. A more subtle threat comes from sandwich crusts scattered on the plateau. These attract crows and gulls, which while they're up there also take ptarmigan eggs and chicks.

From Beinn a' Bhuird the plateau proceeds eastwards in boulder and bog until the sudden drop to the Lairig an Laoigh. Beyond the gap, the plateau is higher, and more harsh.

Above: Ptarmigan on nest

THE CAIRNGORM-MACDUI PLATEAU

Boulderfields and gravel, with snow lying through much of the summer: that's the high plateau of the Cairngorms. Over these smooth slopes wind flows uninterrupted, to reach 170mph (270kph) at the weather station on Cairngorm's summit.

Granite erodes easily into coarse sand, low in minerals. What soil there is gets washed out by rain or blown away. The plants that do grow, grow low. Bearberry and mountain azalea hug the gravel; saxifrage and moss campion form shallow tussocks.

It's tough at the top. Ptarmigan and mountain hare eat what plants there are, while eagle and peregrine pass by on their way to nests in the crags below. And at November's first blizzard, all life leaves the plateau – apart from the odd human in its brightly-coloured specialised outer coating.

Near the summit of Ben Macdui is a ruined hut, built by the surveyors of 1847 who determined that this hill is 100ft (30m) lower than Ben Nevis and so only Britain's second hill. The Earl of Fife planned, but never built, a summit sepulchre for himself of the necessary height. Queen Victoria went up it anyway, by a roundabout and easy-angled route by way of Loch Etchachan. Although this route is gentle enough for her pony Fyvie, it is full of interest. The fine forests of Glen Derry lead into the empty upper valley. The route turns in between the spectacular crags of Coire Etchachan. A well-built path slants up to the loch. Here the boulders slope away, so that the half-mile of water lies open below the wide sky. And there's still an hour of climbing ahead...

Above: Boulderfield on Monadh Mor

LAIRIG GHRU:
THE GREAT PASS OF THE CAIRNGORMS

Glaciers going both ways have carved a hollow through the heart of the Cairngorms. Although the pass reaches a respectable height of 820m (2,700ft) its walls of rotten rock and boulder rise another 300m (1,000ft) again.

This has been a through route from Aviemore to Braemar for cattle drovers and cattle thieves, for fugitives and business people. Women of Rothiemurchus came through laden with eggs for the market of Braemar. It's just as popular with today's walkers and even cyclists. This despite the awkwardness of arranging the return journey: A to B through the pass is just 24 miles (38km), B to A back again is 70 miles (110km) of twisting hill roads, while the return by public transport involves two trains, a bus and a visit to Aberdeen.

Today's walkers set out from the skiers' car park. Much better (but slightly longer) is from Coylumbridge, with the first 4 miles (6km) under the tall pines of Rothiemurchus. The stony path now climbs into the gap that seemed so small from Aviemore. Just beyond the pass are the four small Pools of Dee. They lie among boulderpiles, with neither inlet nor outflow, and are said to retain a year-round temperature of 2°C.

The descending path passes the Clach nan Taillear, or Tailors' Stone. Three tailors accepted a wager to dance on the same day at the Dell of Abernethy, the Dell of Rothiemurchus and Dalmore near Braemar. They danced at the first two dells, but perished in the snow while crossing the pass.

BEN MACDUI'S GREAT GREY MAN

Professor Norman Collie was a respected academic and a more-than-respected mountaineer – Sgurr Thormaid in the Cuillin is named after him. The first man along Collie's Ledge on Sgurr Mhic Choinnich was not easily scared, but he admitted to a disturbing experience on Macdui. Ascending the mountain in thick mist, he heard something walking in the crisp snow behind him. The sound was not an echo: for every three steps of the professor, the thing behind him took just one. Collie's nerve broke, and he fled the mountain.

Others at once disclosed similar experiences: and in fact 'Fear-liath Mor' had been known to the folk of Rothiemurchus for centuries. Later Sir Hugh Rankine, a mountaineer who was also both a Buddhist and a baronet, met a strange being at the Pools of Dee that addressed him in Sanskrit. The most recent encounter was in 1948, when an Aberdonian climber emptied his service revolver in the direction of an uncanny presence near the summit cairn.

Above: Rain-shower approaching along Glen Geusachan. Both its Gaelic name and the bog oak in its peat indicate that this high valley off the Lairig Ghru was once forested

Left: Tors on Bynack More. Here and there across the plateau, granite tors form a resting point for the eye in the smoothly-moving plateau landscape. On days of storm their shelter also provides a resting point for the body... they formed in a period of hot, wet climate that occurred as our continent drifted across the equator 50 million years ago. Their survival indicates that the summit ice cap was almost stationary, unlike the fiercely erosive corrie glaciers around the edges

CAIRN TOUL AND THE GREAT MOSS

Cairn Toul is a hill of two sides. From the Lairig Ghru it rises steep and stony until its ridges converge onto a perfect pointed peak. But from the west it and its companion Braeriach are simply high points at the edge of the fell-field; and it's apparent that before the glacier got to work, there must have stood an even greater summit some 3,000ft (900m) above where the Dee now flows.

The fell-field that it's the corner of is the Moine Mhor, or Great Moss. Six miles (10km) of gently rolling grass, with small and rather dismal lochans: but all around the edge are sudden edges of rock or scree, and long views down to a peaty valley and a river – and at the foot of the valley the start of the forest. With every step westwards across the Great Moss the ground gets emptier: this is a long way from anywhere and very high up, and even in summer it's easy to get lost among the dun hummocks.

Walk quietly, though, and this is where you may well see great herds of deer. Carn Eilrig, a foothill to the north of Braeriach, takes its name from

Above: Loch Einich and the Sgorans on a crisp autumn afternoon

an early form of deer-hunt. 'Eileirg' is a defile where deer were driven into a prepared ambush – in this case, the narrowing valley of the Allt Druidh. Directly opposite, the high crag of Creag an Leth-choin (Lurcher's Crag) commemorates the end to another deer-hunt that ran up onto the plateau corner from Ryvoan, 10 miles away (15km) and 3,000ft (1,000m) below. The aim was to drive the deer against the clifftop and force some of them over the edge; but one of the deer hounds also fell to its death.

The coming of the rifle made possible the gentlemanly sport of deer-stalking, which was invented by the Duke of Bedford around 1850. Those with a distaste for blood sports may take a grim satisfaction in a story from the 1890s. A ghillie was driving a wounded stag off the Great Moss to save the trouble of carrying it down dead on a pony. The stag kicked out, caught the gun with its hoof, and shot the ghillie dead.

Out in the lonely centre of the Moss, the sharp edges and popular summits are left behind. All around are low and little-walked heather hills. The wind whispers in the grasses, and on that wind drifts the occasional eerie cry of the plover. And all the way across there's that uncertainty: is my compass clever enough to get me off this place in the end?

But then a low line of cairns, half-buried in moss, appears on the facing hummock. The ancient path leads over the edge of this particular world, and down through the heather into the shelter of the pines. The day's last light gleams off the wide River Feshie. Between the pine-trunks, a candle gleams in the bothy window.

Above: Cairn Toul above cloud   Right: Deer at Loch Muick, with Cairn Bannoch behind

11 WALKING IN THE HILLS

THE GREAT VALLEYS can be driven round in a car, and you can enter the darkness under the ancient pines in just twenty minutes along a well-made path. But from riverside or forest you're looking up at the high curve of the hill and wondering about the hidden lochs and great rocky corries.

The first two of the walks below are ways to get into the granite ground without having to venture onto the high plateau. The other three are suggested as being even better than the traditional straight march from car park to summit and back. Please note, though, that high-level walks in the Cairngorms (in which I include the Lairig Ghru) are only suitable for experienced walkers who've learnt the basics on lower hills. Getting lost here can be fatal.

Above: The track into Gleann Einich

Opposite: Frozen Loch Insh

GLEANN EINICH (BADENOCH)
14 miles (23km) there and back on paths and tracks; a safe and sheltered route that gives more than a taste of crag, loch and forest.

Start at Loch an Eilein car park. From the east corner of the loch take a path east, signed 'Lairig Ghru'. After ½ mile (1km) at small Lochan Deo turn right on the track into Gleann Einich.

After a mile (2km) a path forks off left, rejoining the track a mile (2km) later. The ford of the Beanaidh Bheag may be impassable after heavy rain or snowmelt, but usually there is a dry-foot crossing a few yards upstream. The walk ends at the foot of Loch Einich, but the path by Coire Dhondail is a fine route onto the Moine Mhor.

LOCH AVON FROM GLENMORE
18 miles (29km) mostly on paths but with one very rough stretch: a serious outing through remote country that takes twice as long as the simple haul over Cairngorm but is more than twice as good.

Start at Heron's Field, Glenmore (river bridge just south of the village). Nature trail leads upstream and past Glenmore Lodge to join a broad track. This leads past Lochan Uaine and through the Pass of Ryvoan to a junction. Take the rough track on the right, signed 'Braemar by Lairig an Laoigh', to reach the basic shelter at Bynack Stable.

A wide path climbs the flank of Bynack More – easy to follow except when snowcovered – to Fords of Avon, where there is another basic shelter. A very rough ill-defined path leads upstream to the foot of Loch Avon. (If the water is low enough for a crossing of the River Avon, the walk can be splendidly extended by a complete circuit of Loch Avon, possibly with an overnight stop at the Shelter Stone.)

A rough path slants up into the Saddle. A clearer path leads down into Strath Nethy, a fine ravine that becomes boggy flats before reaching Bynack Stable.

From the Saddle, mountain alternatives are also possible: either over Bynack More and down its delightful north ridge, or up onto Cairngorm and along the rim of its northern corries.

BEN MACDUI: THE QUEEN'S WAY (UPPER DEESIDE)
19 miles (31km) on paths and tracks: a serious route with 4,000ft (1,200m) of ascent; Ben Macdui's plateau is tricky in mist.

Start at Linn of Dee. Using a bike for the smooth track to Derry Lodge saves about 1½ hours overall. Derry Lodge has an emergency phone and bothy (Bob Scott's).

After the pleasant pines of Glen Luibeg, a short-cut is possible by Luibeg Burn and Sron Riach. Better is to cross the Luibeg Burn (note footbridge 400yd upstream) for the small path up the spur of Carn a' Mhaim. A splendid walk follows down Carn a' Mhaim's north ridge, before the steep pull onto the plateau (small path, then boulderfield). Cross featureless stony ground to Macdui's huge cairn.

Returning eastwards, do not drop left too early into the valley of the Garbh Uisge Mor but find the clear path leading down to Loch Etchachan. From the outflow turn down into spectacular Coire Etchachan, passing the bothy (Hutchison Hut – though Hutchison Hutch would be more appropriate). Well-used path runs down to Derry Lodge.

Queen Victoria used the Etchachan route both outward and back – Carn a' Mhaim is unsuitable for ponies.

LAIRIG GHRU: DEESIDE TO GLEN MORE
21 miles (33km) Linn of Dee to Aviemore Station, on paths: Scotland's classic through-route. The high section through the pass is rough, and can be very windy.

The truly energetic will go for the traditional start at Braemar, which adds 6 miles (9km). Start through Morrone Birkwood to descend forest road to grid ref 119897. From Linn of Corriemulzie a forest track parallels the tarmac to Inverey.

From Linn of Dee, the route by Glen Derry and Glen Luibeg is shorter, and more wooded, than the alternative by White Bridge. The Luibeg Burn

Below: Winter lies late on Ben Macdui. In late May, snowfields lead down to a frozen Loch Etchachan

can be awkward: note the footbridge 400yd upstream. The path rejoins the Dee opposite Corrour Bothy (shelter).

Two miles (3km) after the bothy, walkers have accidentally turned left into the cul-de-sac of the Garbh Coire. After the high pass, note that the Sinclair Hut, marked on older maps, no longer exists. Here the popular route is to fork right through the Chalamain Gap for the ski-slope car park. But Aviemore is a more congenial rendezvous, and the finish through the Rothiemurchus forest is very fine. Turn left at the path junction called Picadilly to cross the Cairngorm Club footbridge. If time pemits, fork left for Loch an Eilein. A small path leads out from Croft to Inverdruie.

Above: 'The crags that are wild and majestic,
The steep frowning glories of dark Lochnagar!'

LOCHNAGAR (LOWER DEESIDE)
14 miles (23km) on paths with a short rough section: this walk combines Dark Lochnagar with the even-darker Dubh Loch.

From Spittal of Glenmuick take tracks and paths westwards to the col by Meikle Pap – do not skirt left of this col, which has a splendid view. (Meikle Pap itself is even better.) Skirt cragtops to the summit of Lochnagar.

The path continues just south of west. Note that point 1110 is a minor Munro called Carn a' Coire Boidheach, and Carn an t-Sagairt Mor is another. Drop into the boggy upper valley of the Allt an Dubh-loch, keeping to the left for dryer ground. As the valley steepens, a small path descends to left of waterfalls.

Pass to left of the Dubh Loch to Loch Muick. The path round the east side of the loch has the better views.

THE LOW-DOWN

Shorter walks in the glens and forests have been mentioned in the main chapters as follows:

BADENOCH

Creag Bheag, Kingussie *page 36*
Insh Marshes *page 40*

GLEN MORE

Craigellachie birchwood, Aviemore *page 47*
Around Loch an Eilein *page 47*
Loch an Eilein and Ord Ban *page 48*

STRATHSPEY

Abernethy forest trails *page 58*
Ellan Wood, Carrbridge *page 58*
Grantown and Spey *pages 59–60*

GLEN AVON AND THE WHISKY HILLS

Glenlivet walks *page 69*
Lecht Mine *page 70*

UPPER DEESIDE

Glen Ey to Colonel's Bed *page 79*
Morrone Birkwood, Braemar *page 82*
Creag Choinnich, Braemar *page 83*
Morrone *page 83*

LOWER DEESIDE

Balmoral waymarked walks *page 87*
Round Loch Muick *page 90*
Craigendarroch, Ballater *page 92*

*Opposite: Loch Muick; the area's largest
loch and the last mile of the Lochnagar
walk*

USEFUL INFORMATION AND PLACES TO VISIT

PLACES WORTH VISITING MENTIONED IN THE TEXT

BADENOCH
Clan Macpherson Museum *page 34*
Highland Folk Museum *page 35*
Ruthven Barracks *page 37*
Insh Marshes (RSPB) *page 40*
Highland Wildlife Park *page 42*
Insh Church, Kincraig *page 42*

GLEN MORE
Craigellachie Nature Reserve *page 47*
Loch an Eilein *page 47*
Reindeer Centre *page 51*
Cairngorm Mountain Experience (funicular) *page 52*

SPEY
Castle Roy *page 55*
Loch Garten Osprey Centre *page 57*
Roches moutonnées, Dulnain Bridge *page 58*
Dell Wood Reserve *page 58*
Landmark, Carrbridge *page 58*
Grantown-on-Spey *page 59*

AVON AND THE WHISKY HILLS
Queen's View *page 64*
Tomintoul *page 64*
Glenlivet Distillery *page 67*

DONSIDE
Well of Lecht and Lecht Mine *page 70*
Corgarff Castle *page 70*
Glenbuchat Castle *page 72*
Kildrummy Castle *page 72*

UPPER DEESIDE
Linn of Dee *page 78*
Linn of Quoich *page 78*
Colonel's Bed *page 79*
Morrone Birkwood *page 82*
Braemar Castle *page 83*

LOWER DEESIDE
Balmoral Castle *page 86*
Falls of Garbh-allt *page 88*
Loch Muick *page 90*
Falls of Muick *page 90*
Ballater *page 91*

TOURIST INFORMATION

Aviemore (year-round): 01479 810363
Braemar (seasonal): 01339 741600

VIRTUAL VISITING

www.highlandfolk.com (Highland Folk Museum)
www.kincraig.com/wildlife (Highland Wildlife Park
    with wolfpack gossip)
www.nethybridge.com/rspb.htm (osprey gossip)
www.crownestate.co.uk/estates/scottish/glenlivet
    (Glenlivet Estate)
www.balmoral-castle.co.uk (Balmoral Castle)
www.phy.hw.ac.uk/resrev/aws/weather.htm
    (Cairngorm summit weather data)

LITERARY VISITING

These are non-specialist books that have increased my own enjoyment and appreciation of the Cairngorms country.

Baxter, Colin and Goodier, Rawden. *Cairngorms – Nature of the Land* (Colin Baxter Photography, 1-900455-72-2, paperback)
His home hills by one of Scotland's leading photographers.

British Geological Survey. *Cairngorms: a Landscape Fashioned by Geology* (SNH, 1-85397-086-7)
A lucid and well-illustrated booklet.

Brockie, Keith. *Mountain Reflections* (Mainstream, 1-85158-557-5)
Ptarmigan and the mountain hare, drawn not photographed, and lovingly described in words as well.

Charles, Prince of Wales, illustrated Sir Hugh Casson KCVO. *The Old Man of Lochnagar* (Picture Puffin, 0-14-054414-3)
Mild adventures along Deeside.

Crumley, Jim. *A High and Lonely Place* (Jonathan Cape, 0-224-02682-8)
The sanctuary and plight of the Cairngorms – poetic and impassioned.

Elizabeth Grant of Rothiemurcus. *Memoirs of a Highland Lady* (Canongate, 0-86241-396-6)
Aristocratic life in the forest.

Miles, Hugh and Jackman, Brian. *The Great Wood of Caledon* (Colin Baxter Photography, 0-948661-26-7)
Affectionate and non-specialist natural history with fine photos.

Mitchell, Ian. *On the Trail of Queen Victoria* (Luath, 0-946487-79-0)
Careful retracing of her various ascents and expeditions. Coming from a Marxist republican, the conclusion that 'Viccy' would have made a not-bad bothy companion is a high tribute.

Queen Victoria. *Leaves from the Journal of our Life in the Highlands* (not in print, most recent edition as *Queen Victoria's Highland Journals* pb Webb and Bower)
The book that created today's middle-class monarchy. Victoria's infectious delight in Deeside expressed itself in hundred-mile pony treks.

Scroggie, Sydney. *The Cairngorms Scene and Unseen* (SMT, 0-907521-25-8)
Hillwalking reminiscences of the post-war years – by a hillwalker who happens to be blind and have only one leg.

Smith, Robert. *25 Walks Deeside* (Mercat Press, 1-84183-00-0)
Low-level walks taking half a day or less. About half are up a valley on a Landrover track and back the same way, but that's the nature of the country.

Walsh, Maurice. *The Key above the Door*
Walsh, Maurice. *The Small Dark Man* (Balnain, 1-872557-13-9 and 19-8)
Romantic fiction where men are men, women are women and the surroundings are the Cairngorms. *Key* is set at Loch an Eilein, *Small Dark Man* is in Glen Avon and at Inchrory.

Watson, Adam. *The Cairngorms, Lochnagar and the Mounth* (SMC, 0-907521-39-8)
Definitive guide for walkers and mountaineers, which also covers rock and ice climbing, natural history etc.

INDEX

Page numbers in *italic* indicate illustrations

Abergeldie, 90–1; Castle, *91*
Abernethy Forest, 55–7, 58
Ailnack Gorge, *65*
Argyll Stone, 67
Aviemore, 13, 44, *44*
Avon, Glen and River, 63–4

Baile Gean, *27, 28, 35*, 35
Ballater, 91–2, *92, 93*
Balmoral Castle, 86–7, *86, 87*
Beinn a' Bhuird, *6, 66*, 79, 95
Beinn Bhrotain, *12*
Ben Avon, 66, 95
Ben Macdui, 97, 104
Black Colonel (John
    Farquarson), 78, 79, 83
black houses, *27, 35*, 35
Black Officer (John
    Macpherson), 40
Bobbing John, 73, 83
Bonnie Prince Charlie, 29, 37,
    70, 76, 83, 90
bothies, *41*, 52, 74
Braemar, *80*, 82; Castle, *83*;
    games, 19
Brown, John, 64, 87–8
Bynack More, *98*, 104
Byron, Lord, 88–90, 91

Cairn Toul, *76*, 99, *100*
Cairngorm, 63, 104; weather sta-
    tion, *7*; funicular, 14, 52–3;
    North Corries, 49, *50*
Cairngorms National Park, 7,
    32, 88
Caledonian pines, *2, 10, 14, 15,
    14–15*, 55–7
capercaillie, 18, 42, 48, *48*
Carn a' Chalamain, *111*
Carrbridge, 58, *59*
Castle Roy, *55*

cattle: droving, 30, 63; theft, 28,
    29, 52
Colonel's Bed, *78*, 79
Comyn, Black Walter, 41
Corgarff Castle, *70*, 70–1
corries, 49
Craig Choinnich, Braemar, 82–3
Craigellachie Reserve, *45*, 47
Craigendarroch, Ballater, 92
Crathie church, 88
Creag Bheag, 35–6
Creag Dubh, 34
crested tit, 58

Dabrach, Aald, 76
Dalwhinnie, *13*, 13
Dee, River, *6*, 9, 30, 74, *75, 76, 77,
    79, 84*, 85, 93
deer, red, 18, 22, 23, 99–100, *101*;
    stalking, 7, 22, 31–2, 100
Dell Wood, 58
Devil's Point, 74, *76*
Don, River, 9, 70
dotterel, 18
Drumin Castle, 67
Dulnain kipper, 59

eagle, 17, 64
Earls of Mar, 82, 83; Bobbing
    John, 73, 83

fairies (sithean) 15, 52
Fife (Earls, Dukes of), 79, 97,
    82–3, 85
fly agaric, *22*
fur trade, 27, 56

Gaick Pass, 40–1
Garbh-allt, falls, *89*
geese, 23, 40
ghosts, 76–8, 90; *see also* spectres

Gleann Einich, *20*, 102, *102, 103*
Glen Ey, *31*, 32
Glen Feshie, *15*, 41, *41*
Glen Geusachan, *99*
Glen Luibeg, *4*
Glenbuchat Castle, 72
Glenlivet: Braes of, 66–7, 69;
    whisky, 67–9
Glenmore village, 49
goldeneye duck, 40
granite, 7, 96–7, *97, 98, 72, 98*
Grant, Clan, 7, 47
Grantown on Spey, 59, *59*
Great Grey Man, Ben Macdui, 97
Great Moss (Moine Mhor)
    99–100
Great Outdoor Challenge, 18
grouse, *18*

hare, mountain, 17, 18
Highland Clearances, 30, *31*,
    35–6
Highland Folk Museum, 35, *35,
    36; see also* Baile Gean
Highland games, 19–22, 72
Highland Wildlife Park, 42,
    42, 48
hill racing, 22, 82–3

Insh Marshes (RSPB), 40
Inverdruie, 47

Kildrummy Castle, *72, 73*, 72–3
Killiecrankie, 12
Kingussie, 35, *36*

Lairig an Laoigh, *51*, 63, 102
Lairig Ghru, *10*, 49, *76*, 97, 102,
    104–5
Lecht, 70, *71*; Well of, *28*;
    ski-ing, 24

Left: Spring birches, Glen Feshie

lichen, *1, 56*
Linn of Dee, *77, 78*
Linn of Muick, falls, 91
Linn of Quoich, 78
Loch an Eilein, *26, 46,* 47–8
Loch Avon, *62,* 63, *94,* 102–4
Loch Einich, *100,* 102
Loch Etchachan, *104*
Loch Garten (RSPB), *57,*
    57–8, 48
Loch Insh, *24,* 41–2
Loch Morlich, 49, *50, 111*
Loch Muick, *19,* 88, 90, 91, *91,*
    101, 106
Lochan Uaine, 15, 51–2
Lochnagar, *84,* 88–90, 105,*105*
lost?, 72
Lowlanders, Great Hatred, 27, 29

Macpherson, Clan, 13, 34–5;
    Green Banner, *34*
Mar Lodge, 79, *79*
military roads, *28,* 28–9, 72
mining, 70, *71*
Monadh Liath, 7, *9*
Monadh Ruadh, 7
Morrone, 82–3; Birkwood, 82
moss campion, *19*
mountaineering, 32, 95
Mrs Brown, 72, 87

National Park, 7, 32, 88

National Trust for Scotland, 7,
    14, 22, 32, 79;
    see also Mar Lodge
Newtonmore, *9,* 34, *34*

Ord Ban, 48
osprey, 18, 47–8, 57–8, *58*

peregrine, 22
porridge, 59, 60
ptarmigan, 96, *96*

Queen's View, Tomintoul, 64

recipes; Earl of Mar's punch, 78;
    porridge, 60
Red Hand, spectre, 49
reindeer, 51
Robert the Bruce, 12, 27, 47,
    72–3
roches moutonneés, 58
Rothiemurchus Forest, *2, 14,*
    15, 48
RSPB, 7; *see also* Insh Marshes,
    Loch Garten
Ruthven Barracks, 28, 37–40,
    37, 38
Ryvoan; bothy, 52;
    Pass, 51–2, 102

salmon, 18, 23, 85–6; *see also*
    Dulnain kipper

schist, *1,* 47, 85
Scottish crossbill, 58
Shelter Stone, 63
shielings, 28
ski-ing, 24, 52–3, *53*
snow bunting, 23, 96
snowpatch, enduring, 22
spectres, 49, 97; *see also* ghosts
Spey, River, *9,* 9, 30, *54, 60*
squirrel, red, *23, 90*
Stevenson, Robert Louis, 83
Strathspey Railway, 44

Tailors' Stone, 97
Thieves' Road, 52, 66
timber trade, 30, *33,* 56, 86
Tomintoul, 64–6, *66*
tormentil, *95*
tors, *98*

Victoria, Queen, 9, *30,* 31–2, 59,
    64, 82, 85–8, 90, 104;
    see also Mrs Brown

weather, bad, 23, *24,* 96
whisky, *13 , 67, 68,* 67–9, 88
White Mounth, 7, 88
whooper swan, 23, 40, 42
wildcat, 42, 56, 57
witchcraft, 41, 90
wolf, *42,* 56
Wolf of Badenoch (Alexander
    Stewart) 66, 47